W9-AFJ-803

WHAT IS CINEMA?
VOLUME II

WHAT IS CINEMA? VOL. II

by ANDRÉ BAZIN

essays selected and translated
by HUGH GRAY

UNIVERSITY OF CALIFORNIA PRESS
Berkeley   Los Angeles   London

UNIVERSITY OF CALIFORNIA PRESS
Berkeley and Los Angeles, California

UNIVERSITY OF CALIFORNIA PRESS, LTD.
London, England

Copyright © 1971 by The Regents of the University of California

First printing, 1971
First Paperback Edition, 1972

ISBN: 0–520–02255–6
Library of Congress Catalog Card No.: 67–18899

The original edition from which this translation has
been made was published in Paris by Editions du Cerf,
under the title *Qu-est-ce que le Cinéma?* The essays
in this first English edition were selected by the
translator, and are published by arrangement with
Editions du Cerf. All rights reserved.

5 6 7 8 9

FOREWORD

by François Truffaut

ANDRÉ BAZIN wrote about film better than anybody else in Europe. From that day in 1948 when he got me my first film job, working alongside him, I became his adopted son. Thereafter, every pleasant thing that happened in my life I owed to him.

He taught me to write about the cinema, corrected and published my first articles, and helped me to become a director. He died only a few hours after I had finished my first day's shooting. When, on being sent for by his friend Père Léger, I arrived at his home in Nogent, he looked up at me but could no longer speak and was in acute pain. The previous evening he had been watching *Le Crime de Monsieur Lange* on television and making notes for the book he was preparing on Jean Renoir.

If I were asked to give a picture of André Bazin the first thing that would occur to me would be a caption from an American magazine: "The most unforgettable character I've met."

André Bazin, like the characters in the plays of Giraudoux, was a creature from the times before Original Sin. Although we all knew him for a good and honest man, his goodness was nevertheless an endless surprise, so abundantly was it manifest. To talk with him was what bathing in the Ganges must be for a Hindu. Such was his generosity of spirit that I sometimes found myself deliberately running down a common acquaintance just for the pleasure of hearing André defend him.

While he had a heart as big as a house he was also logic itself, a being of pure reason and a superlative dialectician. He had complete faith in the power of argument and I have seen him win over the toughest policeman, being helped rather than hindered by a stammer thanks to which he was able to rivet people's attention. He would expose a dishonest argument by first taking over his adversary's thesis, developing it better than had the man himself, and then demolishing it with rigorous logic. Only in the articles of Sartre, whom Bazin particularly admired, does one find a comparable intelligence and similar intellectual honesty.

His chronic physical ill health was paralleled by his constantly surprising moral strength. He would borrow money aloud but lend it with a whisper. In his presence everything became simple, clear, and aboveboard. Since he considered it wicked to ride in a four-seat car all alone, he often picked up three other people at the bus stop in Nogent, whom he would then drop off along his route in Paris. Whenever he and his wife and small son went away for a few weeks he would look about among his innumerable friends for a couple not so comfortably housed to whom he could lend his house, and then find someone to lend his car to.

He loved the cinema, but still more he loved life, people, animals, the sciences, the arts; just before he died he planned to make a short film about the little known romanesque churches of France. He kept all sorts of pets, a chameleon, a parrot, squirrels, tortoises, a crocodile and other creatures I cannot list because I don't know how to spell their names; not long before he died, he had been force-feeding some kind of lizard, an iguana from Brazil, stuffing pieces of hard-boiled egg into its mouth with a little stick. "I'm afraid," he said, "that I'll die before this poor creature does."

Whether the world be good or evil I cannot say, but I am certain that it is men like Bazin who make it a better place. For, in believing life to be good and behaving accordingly, André had a beneficial effect on all who came in contact with him, and one could count on the fingers of one hand those who behaved badly toward him. Everyone who ever talked with him, even if only once, could call him their "best friend," since in meeting him, overwhelmed by such integrity, it was impossible not to give the best that was in one.

André Bazin was too warm a person to allow us to use such hollow phrases about him as "living still" or "still in our midst," and so on. The cruel, the truly desolating, the profoundly sad fact is that he is dead. All we can do is to weep and reread him. Not long ago I came across a passage in a letter of his that characterizes his critical approach: "I'm sorry I couldn't see Mizoguchi's films again with you at the Cinémathèque. I rate him as highly as you people do and I claim to love him the more because I love Kurosawa too, who is the other side of the coin: would we know the day any better if there were no night? To dislike Kurosawa because one loves Mizoguchi is only the first step toward understanding. Unquestionably anyone who prefers Kurosawa must be incurably blind but anyone who loves only Mizoguchi is one-eyed. Throughout the arts there runs a vein of the contemplative and mystical as well as an expressionist vein."

CONTENTS

TRANSLATOR'S INTRODUCTION

FOUR YEARS AGO in his foreword to the first English volume of *What is Cinema?* Jean Renoir spoke of the influence that André Bazin would undoubtedly exercise in the years ahead. The truth of this is already being borne out in various ways and places. In English-speaking countries, for example, his name appears increasingly in critical studies of film. In France his continued importance as an authority to be reckoned with has again been recognized by the fact that some Marxist film critics seem to have felt it essential to return to the attack against his theories with something of the urgency—if not with quite the same vituperation—yet with the identical arguments of the original assault in the pages of *Positif* in 1962: a protracted invective spread over two issues and running to approximately eighty pages. (They considered it their duty, they said—with the help of words like "charlatan" and "naif"—to "demystify a pope"!)

Paradoxical though it may sound in speaking of a critic whose work at first reading appears so cerebral, the key to any true understanding of the man and his work is the word love—spurned by *Positif* as a catch-all, a term of mystification. "He loved the cinema," François Truffaut tells us in his foreword, "but more than the cinema, he loved life, people, animals, science, the arts."

In the commemorative number of *Cahiers du Cinéma* that appeared after Bazin's death, Truffaut likened him to a "companion of St. Francis of Assisi possessed of a kind of goodness at once comical and touching."

Nothing could illustrate this better than the charming and humorous article that appeared in *Cahiers* (January, 1959) after his return to France from a film festival in South America, in which he describes his efforts, happily successful in spite of every official and unofficial obstacle, to bring home a parrot.

In the same commemorative issue of *Cahiers,* Claude Vermorel also spoke of Bazin's "natural Franciscan goodness." The significance of these comparisons extends to something far beyond their surface meaning as can be seen, for example, from his essays on neorealism and from the importance he attaches to the recurrent (and, for his opponents, objectionably "idealist") phrase "respect for reality." If I were making a film of his life I would open on a significantly associative or symbolic shot of Bazin in his critical, beginning twenties, as he crosses the square in front of St. Sulpice, a large and somber-looking structure and long the embodiment of all that was somber and solemn about traditional French Catholicism. The name of the church is additionally significant since it was adopted by a congregation of priests of which his friend and colleague Amedée Ayfre would later become a member. Bossuet and Fénelon, equally symbolic seventeenth-century churchmen, stare frozenly down at him as he moves, his mind full of what they would consider theologically revolutionary ideas, toward his destination, the Café St. Sulpice. Gathered there at one of their regular editorial meetings are a group of writers who form part of the staff of *Esprit,* a literary review founded in 1932 to which André later contributed regularly, between 1949 and 1957. Among those present are the Catholic P.-A. Touchard and the Protestant—some say the non-believer—Roger Leenhardt, the one a writer, the other also a film maker, both to become close friends of Bazin. We might find there, too, Bazaine the painter and two distinguished men of the theater, Jacques Coppeau and Dullin, the author of an unusual autobiographical study of acting for both stage and screen, *Souvenirs et notes de travail d'un acteur.*

This would be no invented movie scene. Such a meeting actually took place some time during the period immediately preceding World War II. Bazin had come to meet Touchard with whom he had been in correspondence, at the latter's invitation, to make his formal acquaintance and to discuss the Esprit group which Bazin had founded at the *Ecole Normal Supérieure* at St. Cloud, where he was training to be a teacher. These groups, centers for philosophical, theological, and sociological discussion, were encouraged and supported by the French Personalist movement, the guiding spirit and main driving force behind which was Emmanuel Mounier (1905-1950). When writing later of Bazin, Touchard referred to Mounier as "their common master from whom Bazin had acquired his almost invincible passion for abstract terminology." But he had acquired more than that from Mounier.

Bazin has left no specific philosophical testament but it appears like a watermark (to use a favorite comparison of his) in the texture of his writings and the more we examine this texture the more we see what Touchard meant when he called Mounier their common master, although one feels that it is not a case of a pupil learning at the knee, but rather of a mind that had found its fellow. The philosophy of Mounier is a variation of the Personalist movement that existed in different forms in France, the United States, England, Holland, Switzerland, and elsewhere. Its approach to life, to man and to his place in the cosmos and society and to his relations with his fellows, was initially developed while Mounier was at the University of Grenoble, his native city. Its basis was the affirmation of the existence of free and creative persons and it introduces into the structure of its thought the idea of the unforeseen which naturally rules out any desire for definitive systemization. "Nothing," Mounier wrote, "is more repugnant than the fondness so common nowadays for a machine to think and act for us, an automatic distributor of solutions and recommendations; such a thing is a barrier to research, an insurance against disquiet (*Angst*) or any sort of self-testing or the taking of risks." In order therefore to get away from the idea of Personalism as a rigid system he suggests that one should avoid talking of Personalism; rather one should think of it in the plural, that is of personalisms—Christian, agnostic, and so on. One can readily see how this openness, this pluralistic tone, with its sense of individual freedom so evidently reflected in Bazin's writings, must irk his Marxist critics.

The thinkers who most influenced Mounier were the Russian Berdiaeff, Bergson, Bergson's former pupil the neo-Thomist Jacques Maritain, but above all Charles Peguy (1873-1914), a poet, an ardent Catholic, and an equally ardent socialist who inscribed his first book *Jeanne d'Arc* to "those women and men who have dedicated their lives to the establishment of the world-wide socialist republic."

In 1932, when he launched *Esprit,* Mounier summed up the position of the movement as follows: "We are looking for a camping ground somewhere between Bergson and Peguy, Maritain and Berdiaeff, Prudhon and deMan." At that time, as Daniel de Rops the historian describes them, they were a generation without masters, trying to break free from the lesser masters of literature they had followed at the University and ignorant as yet of the works of Kierkegaard, Marx and Jaspers. But this was to change and later Mounier was to write that "the task of our age will be perhaps not to try in vain to heal the seemingly unhealable breach that now exists between the followers of Kierkegaard and Marx but to attempt to retrace our steps to the moment of what might be called the Socratic revolution of the nineteenth century, the assault on all the forces of the time that were attempting to depersonalize man. This assault unfortunately separated into two, one went in the direction taken by Kierkegaard recalling contemporary man, dazzled by the discovery and exploitation of the world, to an awareness of his subjectivity and his freedom; the other way was taken by Marx who denounced the processes of mystification in which man had been caught up by a social structure that had been grafted onto his material condition and reminded him, instead, that his destiny lay not only with his heart but with his hands." It was a deplorable division that could only continue to grow wider. Personalism was then to attempt somehow to nullify this, to be the "third force" placed between capitalism and communism, detesting the former and sharing many ideas in common with the latter.

Mounier admired the writings of Teilhard de Chardin who, he said, had restored a cosmic perspective to the Christian message. He was likewise much concerned with existentialism. "Personalism and existentialism," he said, "agree about one thing in particular, the struggle against the system" and he called Personalism a branch of the existential tree. It is a philosophy of existence before being a philosophy of essence, an idea which is echoed *passim* in Bazin, for example in the essay on neorealism: "They (the neorealist directors) never forget that the world *is*, before it is something to be condemned" (p. 21). Capitalism was one of Mounier's main targets. For him it was odious and inhuman and his criticism of it is said to be superior to that of Marx. He denounced the compromise Christians have made with it. He likewise agreed with Peguy that the bourgeoisie in leaving aside grandeur for tranquility had allowed itself to be eaten away by a mortal malady and had corrupted the people. Like Bernanos, he observed that its chief fault was to inject into every level of society "the worst of poisons, namely, mediocrity" (*Moix*. E. Mounier, Editions du Seine, Paris, 1960).

I have dwelled at some length on these various ideas of the "master" since without a minimum, at least, of Personalist philosophy before him the reader will not know what soil it was that nourished Bazin's theory of cinema and his aesthetics, his vision of the world and of society, or of ideals that inspired him—nor will they be aware how unjustified and ill-informed is the shallow "odium theologicum" of his Marxist critics.

The fervor of the disciple had been early evident to Touchard in the energy Bazin devoted to the *Esprit* group at the Ecole Normale at St. Cloud and also to a second group that he had set up during a summer vacation at La Rochelle, two members of which were a revolutionary young abbé and a Protestant pastor.

That his fervor lasted we see from various pieces of evidence, for example in his review in *Esprit* of *Lousiana Story* ten years or so later, in which he insists that his readers see the film. If they do not go or if they do not at least make a firm resolve to go, then they are not worthy to be readers of *Esprit*. A friend of his young days recalls, in the course of a touching obituary poem, how Bazin as a student helped to circulate "underground" copies of the writings of Teilhard de Chardin whose works were banned from publication by his ecclesiastical superiors for fear of their possible unorthodoxy. Who, reading Bazin or de Chardin, can fail to hear some of the ideas and even some of the vocabulary echoing from one to the other?

5

What was it that drew this young man to the cinema, his enthusiasm for which has been described as part of his passion for culture, for the truth? Bearing in mind what we have just outlined of the philosophy that appeared to attract him, and likewise his own exquisitely sensitive awareness of the beauty of the landscape of the world and of all it contains, I think it would not be wrong to conclude that the attraction in great part lay in the camera's special relation to all of this, to life and movement, to reality. It permitted him in a special way to dwell on everything he prized. As he himself said, "The cinema more than any other art is bound up with love." Small wonder then that he immersed himself in it, eagerly followed its evolution, and resisted any abuse of an instrument that permitted him the thrill of following this ever-moving "asymptote"—a word he characteristically borrowed from mathematics—that must reach out to, yet ever fall short of that "realism" that would be its own destruction.

These speculations arise not unnaturally from an ever closer study of his writing. What is not speculation is the influence of the man who shared with François Truffaut his dedication of the first volume of his collected essays—Roger Leenhardt. Jean Louis Tellaney says that "Bazin was conquered by Leenhardt who was passionately devoted to the cinema" and this is also the view of Georges Sadoul. We have Bazin's own assessment of Leenhardt as the man who wrote with the most subtlety about the cinema. We have, finally, the testimony of Leenhardt himself. "He [Bazin] was kind enough to say that my column in *Esprit* where he replaced me had influenced him in his vocation as a critic." One of the reasons, and not the least of them, that led Leenhardt to give up writing about the cinema "without regret" was that what Bazin wrote "was a continuation of what I was doing and he took it beyond what I was trying to do."

Certainly, from Bazin's review of Leenhardt's *Dernières vacances,* a most deft handling of the art of making gentle criticism seem like warm praise, it is evident how far the pupil had advanced and what an accomplished critic he had already become by the time he took over Leenhardt's column and became a regular member of the *Esprit* staff of contributors.

Leenhardt also tells us that Bazin was impressed and to some extent influenced by Malraux's now famous essay *Sketch for a Psychology of the Motion Picture* (*Verve,* Vol. V, No. 2, 1940). The likeness between some of the ideas in this essay and Bazin's *Ontology of the Photographic Image* is marked. Both are concerned with the art of painting as distinct from the technique of representation. Both speak in substance of the cinema as the natural climax to what Malraux describes as the "frantic headlong quest of movement by the votaries of representation at the end of the baroque period." Both use the comparison of an "identity card." There appear, however, to be points of divergence notably on the transition from the silent to the talking picture as discussed by Bazin in another essay. The references common to both critics that are reflected in these pages are to cinema and myth, particularly as they relate to Chaplin and to Bazin's analysis of *Monsieur Verdoux*.

So widespread does Bazin's reading seem that an addict of the hallowed process of *Forschungsquellen* might produce all kinds of parallels even from so far afield as *de Rerum Natura* of Lucretius and his theory of images.

At the editorial meetings of *Esprit* Bazin's presence was strongly felt. "There was a daimon in this fellow," a colleague wrote after Bazin's death, "who could make people normally bored with cinema fall in love with it. When he arrived at an editorial meeting its tone would change and the subject under discussion take on a different shape. Automatically everyone would start talking film. But actually we were just spectators and Bazin made no attempt to convince us of the truth of what he was saying. Just by his being there we felt that what we were searching for in current events, even the most trivial ones, the bits and pieces of news or of political arguments, the details of our day-to-day existence, all was to be found in that troubled pool that reflected the changing world of the twentieth century."

Of the essays in this volume those on eroticism and on the western together with the one on Gabin are from the third volume of his collected works entitled *Cinema and Sociology*. The rest are from the fourth volume, *Neorealism: An Aesthetic of Reality*. The western attracted Bazin early, in particular for what it revealed to him of the history and sociology of the West, and characteristically he sees similarities between the cowboy and the knight of courtly French literature and between the women in the new West placed by force of social circumstances upon a pedestal, and the idealized woman of courtly love. Although the statement with which he introduces his "Notes on Eroticism in the Cinema" (once more become singularly relevant) may appear less than prophetic any judgment of his views will depend to some extent on whether one agrees that the nude productions of today—their content naturally affected by their form —are theater according to the common and traditional meaning of that word, and what the role of the actor is therein. In any event it is difficult to believe that if Bazin were writing today his own views would have changed and for two reasons. First, they seem to be firmly rooted in the conception of the actor's role as set forth by Diderot in *Le Paradoxe du comédien,* namely that his function is to stir the public without experiencing the emotions himself and, secondly, that making love like death cannot be performed for another. They are moments uniquely to be lived through and cannot, by definition, be treated as "objects." It is interesting, from another point of view, to see how Bazin distinguishes between the impact of nudity on the stage and on the screen, the effect of the former being more powerful since it is in an actual place. The nude on the screen on the other hand is in an imaginary place. Does not this argue some modification ten years later of his earlier views on the essence of the theater? ("Theater and Cinema," *What Is Cinema?* Vol. 1, p. 95.)

There is a quality present in some of these essays, particularly in "The Outlaw" and "The Entomology of the Pin-up Girl" and also in much of Bazin's other work that, to the best of my knowledge, is never alluded to— his humor. Unfortunately his admirers tend to praise him with solemn intensity while his detractors excommunicate him with whatever is the solemn Marxist equivalent of bell, book, and candle. Thus the grasp of both on the quintessential Bazin is weakened.

His capacity to bring a dialectical brilliance (in the scholastic not the Hegelian sense) to the defense of lost causes or at least of causes in great need of friends is admirably illustrated in his superb analysis of *Limelight* and *Monsieur Verdoux.* The masterly essay on Verdoux is developed from an article that appeared originally in *Les Temps Modernes,* (December, 1947). It was in reply to an unfavorable review of the film by Natalie

Moffat, also printed in *Les Temps Modernes* (July, 1947) which was the second of two articles by her on the film, the first describing its actual production, after she had visited the Chaplin studios. Bazin had seen the film in Czechoslovakia and found that the Czechs had had the same reaction to it as Natalie Moffat. "The Marxists," he said, "regretted the absence of any socially useful lesson."

Charles Brémond, reviewing Bazin's third volume of essays in the first number of *Communication,* a publication of the *Centre d'Etudes des Communications de Masse,* founded just prior to the publication of these essays, praises it as a mine of suggestions, some of them daring and paradoxical but all of them stimulating, to be regarded, however, as the work of a critic not of a sociologist. Thus he calls it a philosophy of the social order rather than sociology. It raises the question, he says, of the relation of sociology and aesthetics, the former being descriptive, the latter normative. He is particularly disturbed by the handling of the myth of Verdoux. To grasp the dialectical relation between Charlie and Verdoux, he argues, is beyond the reach of the general public. For them the only myth is the myth of Charlie. This myth alone has been the real box-office attraction. *Limelight* and *Verdoux* were failures. Only the exceptional eye of Bazin could establish the Charlie-Verdoux relationship. He does admit, however, that the notion is ingenious, even plausible. So, perhaps he has answered his own question and in the years since this review appeared there has grown up a widespread understanding of the Charlie-Verdoux relationship.

In addition to the subject matter that is their main concern, the essays of Bazin are uniformly rich in what might be called parenthetical insights, in associations of ideas, that derive from a combination of wide reading and a synthetic spirit. The essays on neorealism are no exception. The comparison he so adroitly draws for example between the novels of the American critical realists and the neorealist directors argues a penetrating grasp of the literary scene in both countries. Above all, these essays shed an important light on Bazin's attitude on the question of "montage as against depth of focus." He thought the debate had died down and said so in an article in the first number of *Cahiers du Cinéma* entitled "A Final Word About Depth of Focus" (April, 1951). Nobody talked about it anymore,

9

he said, because it had become common practice. In a pertinent passage he explains how in a scene in *The Little Foxes* Wyler had placed a metal box containing important documents in such a position relative to the two characters in the scene that no one could miss its importance. Montage would have shown all this in a series of cuts. "In other words," says Bazin, "the single-shot sequence as used by directors today does not renounce montage—how could it without returning cinema to a state of primitive jibbering?—it makes montage part of the structure of the film."

Bazin did not live to see that his "final word" about depth of focus was nothing of the sort. M. Gozlan of the staff of *Positif* saw to this on the occasion of the publication of the collected essays. Reviewing them in the protracted article to which I referred above and sarcastically entitled "Eulogy for André Bazin," he deals at length in an attack on the whole of Bazin's "system," particularly with what is "rightly or wrongly the best-known part of Bazin's system, his critique of montage." The ultimate source of this and of everything else is reputed to be Christian theology and Bazin, presumably an "opiate" addict, is dismissed as a bourgeois idealist. The ambiguity which Bazin posits in the face of reality and of the cinematic image of reality is ridiculed alike in the text and in the title of the first installment "The Delights of Ambiguity."

The most recent revival of the controversy was in *Les Temps Modernes* (December, 1970) in an article entitled "All Films are Political," in which Christian Zimmer attempts to lay the foundations for a new criticism of cinema which would call for the elimination of any notion of the film image as an "impression of reality." In their concern to give film a cultural status the critics had overlooked, it seems, the economic process in film production. All films therefore made under capitalism are inescapably bourgeois including those made with the best of proletarian intentions.

Hitherto most critics, being men of letters, have treated cinema as if it were literature. This, according to Zimmer, is the idealist approach and the foremost representative of that approach is Bazin. His theory and that of his followers rest upon one simple fallacy—the transparence of the cinematic spectacle, the fallacy of seeing the screen as a mirror or a window open onto the world, with, in consequence, intimations of the invisible and, by inference, of the spiritual. This fallacy is the basis for Bazin's phobia about montage. He is confusing the thing represented with the representation. The image is not a fragment of reality, it is the produce of labor. Labor makes use of reality as an ingredient in the process, but this process does not render reality back in its original purity. Thus the obsession of Bazin with concrete reality is in line with the broad tradition of bourgeois humanism which sees in painstaking and preconceived realism the ideal of the artist, in other words a kind of photographic prowess for its own sake. The solution is to escape from this reality-related system, to speak with a "class tongue" and forget that figment of the commercial imagination "the public." Most importantly, it would seem, concern for the impression of reality neutralizes the subversive power of the film.

Clearly here, as with all the arguments used by these critics to attack the views of Bazin, we are faced with Mounier's "unhealable breach." Short of taking the discussion back step by step to the historical and material dialectic from which they derive and beginning the argument from there, there is no way to deal with them, for they are arguments put forward not on their own intrinsic merits but from authority. For the rest, one is left only to deplore the treatment accorded by them to the works of a critic who approached the cinema with a rich sense of the elusive paradoxes of art and hence of aesthetics. One wonders indeed if Gozlan or Zimmer have truly examined their subject.

If they had, how can they talk of him, against the clear evidence both of Bazin's own writings and of the philosophy of Personalism which he shared, and which I purposely outlined at some length, as bourgeois and presumably the dupe, as they would call it, of capitalist ideology? Again, if they had, they surely would have shown a fuller understanding of his position in the argument over montage and depth of focus.

Furthermore why do they insist on seeing in his concept of "reality" and of the cinema's obligation to respect reality only an indication of the mental subservience of Bazin the pious Catholic? In fact, its antecedents date back five centuries before the Christian era. Have they never heard of the philosopher Xenophanes who, gazing up at the heavens, proclaimed "the all is one"? Or of Parmenides who saw this whole as a continuum? Indeed if there had been cinema in those days one could imagine a similar argument to the present one going on between the schools of Parmenides and Heraclitus. It was these philosophers who first saw the cosmos or "reality" as a whole. For Plato it was a structured whole, the parts of which are held together by the force of love. Bazin then, the "pious Catholic," is in splendid philosophical company, the company not only of Plato but of the Stoics with their cosmic piety, of Boethius, of Sallustius, to cite but some of the ancients. It is a tradition likewise that saw this world, and all that is in it, as good and as such to be loved. "Everything exists," said Sallustius, using a Platonic argument, "because of some goodness in it." The first cause of all is the Good.

As for ambiguity—is there no mystery about the very concept of matter? No ambiguity? When Lenin proclaims that matter is infinite in itself and exists eternally is he not proclaiming a mystery as unfathomable as if he had substituted the word God for matter?

Bazin had a strong and subtle sense of the evolution of the techniques in the use of which reality is "respected." They are the instruments of an art dedicated to reality—an art of which he used the word "asymptote," perhaps the most illuminating of the words he borrows from the sciences. For him a paradox lay behind this word, the paradox of a realism that is profoundly aesthetic. Paradox indeed is truly the essence not only of his style, but of his mental processes. It is his own particular dialectic which, like his humor, it is dangerous to overlook.

Jean Mitry, to whom Gozlan and Zimmer turn for support, in reality stands somewhere between them and Bazin. He disagrees with the manner in which Bazin predicates reality of the image, but when one reads all he has to say one feels that while his rational processes lead him to this conclusion, something inside him, a less purely analytical sense of cinema, inclines him in Bazin's direction. The filmic image, says Mitry, gives us an arbitrary, not a true, reality. It is not an exact image of the real. Reality is fragmented by camera angles, framing, points of view that arrange these fragments according to relative periods of duration and endow them with a meaning other than that which they had as part of the universal decor. Relations between them now exist that were not present in the original and true reality. From this there results a discontinuous spatio-temporal development different from the real space-time continuum, a statement that seems to explain why Zimmer calls Mitry to witness.

Bazin's reply would be to agree that of course *some* kind of transformation takes place and by this, if one may here insert a gloss, he would mean the kind of change that is implied in the concept of *mimesis* as it has come down to us from Aristotle's *Poetics* when we relate it to cinema. He would repeat what he has said about ellipsis as used for example by Rossellini in the presentation of events, about the filtering of reality through the director's consciousness, a concept which gives rise to his assertion that there is no such thing properly speaking as neorealism. There are only neorealist directors whether they be materialists, Christians, Communists, or whatever. The essential thing is that in this mimetic process there be no cheating on reality however the process of "imaging" is carried out.

"The reality produced by the cinema at will and which it *organizes* is the reality of the world of which we are part and of which the film receives a mold at once spatial and temporal." The word *"organizes"* shows that he accepts the idea of some kind of change, of artifice in short. Did not Bazin say—in praise of Eisenstein's *Potemkin*, no less—that there is no art without artifice and that one must sacrifice something of reality in the process of achieving it?

Mitry on the other hand prefers to talk not of the "coefficient of reality" in the image but of the "coefficient of unreality," of a strange quality which he admits may give a handle to the spiritually inclined. However, such a feeling is not justified, he says, arising as it does simply from the phenomenon of perception. And what is more magical, may one ask, more mystifying than the act of perception? So much for the purely philosophizing Mitry. On the final page of the second volume of his *Esthetique du Cinéma,* however, he takes a definite step, it seems to me, in Bazin's direction: "If the cinema is an art it is an art created in the face of every restriction imposed on art. Certainly art is a pathway to transcendence [sic] but it owes it to itself to lead the way there rather than just to reproduce it and to lead the way via immanence and liberty. Only the cinema can do this, for its prime element is life itself!"

So far we have discussed only the French situation. Bazin's "Defense of Rossellini" is evidence that there were (and there still are) confrontations in Italy. Rossellini also bore witness to this in an interview in *Cahiers* (July, 1954) in which he said that at that time the political struggle had become so feverish that people were no longer free to make judgments and directors were dictated to by their political beliefs. This was a particularly unsatisfactory state of affairs for him, since, as he said, "It is primarily from the moral viewpoint that I look at the world, only later does it become an aesthetic viewpoint" (a statement strangely reminiscent of one of Lenin's: "Today's ethic will be tomorrow's aesthetic").

At the time he was making *Open City* there was, Rossellini said, "a tremendous need for truth. I always respect neorealism for that. We were maintaining a moral position more than a style." This was Bazin's view. It was a Marxist, Ugo Barbaro, who coined the word neorealism, however, and it was the Marxists who were its films' first critics. No actual definition of the word was ever established and a congress at Parma in December, 1952, called to try and arrive at one, failed to do so.

I spoke earlier of love as the key to an understanding of Bazin's writings. I said also that his friends saw in him a likeness to Francis of Assisi. I also said that this association carried a special significance. Nowhere is this more apparent than in the essays on neorealism. It seems to give him a peculiar insight into the films of Rossellini, De Sica, and Fellini and into the writings of Zavattini. For Bazin, *La Strada* was of Franciscan inspiration. Of De Sica and Zavattini's *Bicycle Thief* he writes, "Its true meaning lies in not betraying the essence of things, in allowing them first to exist for their own sakes, freely; it is to love them in their single individual reality. 'My . . . little sister reality,' says De Sica, and she circles about him like the birds around St. Francis. Others put her in a cage or teach her to talk, but De Sica talks to her and it is the true language of reality, that we hear, the word that cannot be denied, that only love can express." Bazin has said he was no philosopher. He could never have denied, however, that he was a poet. What indeed could put more clearly his values, which St. Francis himself long ago foreshadowed in his immortal *Canticle of All Created Things,* which Mounier called "a beautiful piece of medieval realism":

Be praised my Lord with all your creatures especially master brother Sun who brings day, and you give light by him and he is fair and radiant with a great shining and he draws his meaning most high from you . . .

Be praised my Lord for sister moon and the stars in heaven . . . for brother wind . . . and for the air . . . for sister our mother earth . . .

Today we inevitably ask what would Bazin be offering us now from the treasury of his paradoxes?

One, perhaps the greatest of all, has been preserved for us by a colleague of his writing of him in *Esprit* after his death: "Has he not declared that the year 2000 will salute the advent of a cinema free of the artificialities of montage, renouncing the role of an 'art of reality' so that it may climb to its final level on which it will become once and for all 'reality made art' "—perhaps in the way he forsees it in the concluding sentence of his essay on *Umberto D*.

It now remains for me to thank all those to whom I had recourse with problems of translation. In particular may I thank Professor Stephen Werner of the French Department at the University of California, Los Angeles, for his invaluable help. Likewise my good friend and editor Ernest Callenbach for his endless patience and his skillful editorial hand always gloved in the velvet of his tact.

H. G.

AN AESTHETIC
OF REALITY: NEOREALISM

*(Cinematic Realism
and the Italian School of the Liberation)*

THE HISTORICAL importance of of Rossellini's film *Paisà* has been rightly compared with that of a number of classical screen masterpieces. Georges Sadoul has not hesitated to mention it alongside *Nosferatu, Die Nibelungen,* or *Greed.* I subscribe wholeheartedly to this high praise as long as the allusion to German expressionism is understood to refer to the level of greatness of the film but not to the profound nature of the aesthetics involved. A better comparison might be with the appearance in 1925 of *Potemkin.* For the rest, the realism of the current Italian films has been frequently contrasted with the aestheticism of American and, in part, of French productions. Was it not from the outset their search for realism that characterized the Russian films of Eisenstein, Pudovkin, and Dovjenko as revolutionary both in art and politics, in contrast to the expressionist aestheticism of the German films and Hollywood's mawkish star worship? *Paisà, Sciuscà,* and *Roma Città Aperta,* like *Potemkin,* mark a new stage in the long-standing opposition between realism and aestheticism on the screen. But history does not repeat itself; we have to get clear the particular form this aesthetic quarrel assumes today, the new solutions to which Italian neorealism owed its triumph in 1947.

The Precursors

Confronted with the originality of the Italian output, and in the enthusiasm engendered by the surprise that this has caused, we have perhaps neglected to go deeply into the origins of this renaissance, preferring to see it rather as something spontaneously generated, issuing like a swarm of bees from the decaying corpses of fascism and the war. There is no question that the Liberation and the social, moral, and economic forms that it assumed in Italy have played a decisive role in film production. We shall return to this later. It was simply a lack of information about the Italian cinema that trapped us into believing in a sudden miracle.

It could well be that, today, Italy is the country where the understanding of film is at its highest, to judge by the importance and the quality of the film output. The Centro Sperimentale at Rome came into existence before our own Institut des Hautes Etudes Cinématographiques; above all, intellectual speculation in Italy is not, as it is in France, without its impact on film-making. Radical separation between criticism and direction no more exists in the Italian cinema than it does in France in the world of literature.

Furthermore, fascism which, unlike Nazism, allowed for the existence of artistic pluralism, was particularly concerned with cinema. One may have reservations about the connection between the Venice film festival and the political interests of the Duce but one cannot deny that the idea of an international festival has subsequently made good, and one can measure its prestige today by the fact that five or six European countries are vying for the spoils. The capitalists and the Fascist authorities at least provided Italy with modern studios. If they turned out films which were ridiculously melodramatic and overly spectacular, that did not prevent a handful of bright men, smart enough to shoot films on current themes without making any concessions to the regime, from making high-quality films that foreshadowed their current work. If during the war we had not been, albeit justifiably, so prejudiced, films like *SOS 103* or *La Nave Bianca* of Rossellini might have caught our attention more. In addition, even when capitalist or political stupidity controlled commercial production completely, intelligence, culture, and experimental research took refuge in publications, in film archive congresses, and in making short films. In 1941, Lattuada, director of *Il Bandito* and, at the time, the head of the Milan archive, barely escaped jail for showing the complete version of *La Grande Illusion*.*

Beyond that, the history of the Italian cinema is little known. We stop short at *Cabiria* and *Quo Vadis,* finding in the recent and memorable *La Corona di ferro* all the proof we need that the supposed characteristics of films made beyond the Alps remain unchanged: a taste, and a poor taste at that, for sets, idealization of the principal actors, childish emphasis on acting, atrophy of *mise en scène,* the dragging in of the traditional paraphernalia of *bel canto* and opera, conventional scripts influenced by the theater, the romantic melodrama and the *chanson de geste* reduced to an adventure story. Undoubtedly too many Italian films do their best to justify such a caricature and too many directors, including some of the best, sacrificed themselves, sometimes with self-irony, to commercial necessity. The great spectacles like *Scipio Africanus* were, of course, the primary export. There was another artistic vein, however, almost exclusively reserved for the home market. Today, when the thunder of the charging elephants of Scipio is only a distant rumble, we can the better lend an ear to the discreet but delightful sounds made by *Quattro passi fra le nuvole.*

The reader, at least one who has seen this latter film, will undoubtedly be as surprised as we were to learn that this comedy with its unfettered sensibility, brimming over with poetry, the lightly handled socialist realism of which is directly related to the recent Italian cinema, was shot in 1942, two years after the famous *La Corona di ferro* and by the same director: Blasetti, to whom, about the same time, we owe *Un'avventura di Salvator Rosa* and most recently *Un Giorno nella vita.* Directors like Vittorio De Sica who made the admirable *Sciuscià* were always concerned to turn out human and sensitive comedies full of realism, among them, in 1942, *I Bambini ci guardano.* Since 1932, Camerini has made *Gli uomini che*

---

* The influence of Jean Renoir on the Italian cinema is paramount and definitive. Only that of René Clair in any way approaches it.

mascalzoni, the action of which, like *Roma Città Aperta,* is laid in the streets of the capital and *Piccolo Mondo Antico,* no less typically Italian.

As a matter of fact, there are not so many new names among the directors in Italy today. The youngest, like Rossellini, started to make films at the beginning of the war. Older directors, like Blasetti and Mario Soldati, were already known in the early days of the talkies.

But let us not go from one extreme to the other and conclude that there is no such thing as a new Italian school. The realist trend, the domestic, satirical, and social descriptions of everyday life, the sensitive and poetic verism, were, before the war, minor qualities, modest violets flowering at the feet of the giant sequoias of production. It appears that from the beginning of the war, a light began to be shed on the papier-maché forests. In *La Corona di ferro* the style seems to parody itself. Rossellini, Lattuada, Blasetti were striving toward a realism of international importance. Nevertheless it is the Liberation that set these aesthetic trends so completely free as to allow them to develop under new conditions that were destined to have their share in inducing a noticeable change in direction and meaning.

The Liberation: Rupture and Renaissance

Some components of the new Italian school existed before the Liberation: personnel, techniques, aesthetic trends. But it was their historical, social, and economic combination that suddenly created a synthesis in which new elements also made themselves manifest.

Over the past two years, Resistance and Liberation have furnished the principal themes, but unlike the French, and indeed one might say unlike the European cinema as a whole, Italian films have not been limited to themes of the Resistance. In France, the Resistance immediately became legendary. Recent as it was, on the day of the actual Liberation it already belonged to the realm of history. The Germans having departed, life began again. By contrast, in Italy the Liberation did not signify a return to the old and recent freedom; it meant political revolution, Allied occupation, economic and social upheaval. The Liberation came slowly through endless months. It had a profound effect on the economic, social, and moral life of the country. Thus, in Italy, Resistance and Liberation, unlike the Paris uprising, are in no sense just words with a historical connotation. When Rossellini made *Paisà,* his script was concerned with things actually happening at the time. *Il Bandito* showed how prostitution and the black market developed on the heels of the advancing army, how disillusion and lack of employment turned a liberated prisoner into a gangster. Except for unmistakable Resistance films like *Vivere in Pace* or *Il Sole Sorge Ancora,* the Italian cinema was noted for its concern with actual day-to-day events. The French critics had not failed to emphasize (whether in praise or blame but always with solemn surprise) the few specific allusions to the postwar period that Carné deliberately introduced into his last film. If the director and his writer took so much trouble to make us understand this, it is because nineteen out of twenty French films cannot be dated within a decade. On the other hand, even when the central scene of the script is not concerned with an actual occurrence, Italian films are first and foremost reconstituted reportage. The action could not unfold in just any social context, historically neutral, partly abstract like the setting of a tragedy, as so frequently happens to varying degrees with the American, French, or English cinema.

As a result, the Italian films have an exceptionally documentary quality that could not be removed from the script without thereby eliminating the whole social setting into which its roots are so deeply sunk.

This perfect and natural adherence to actuality is explained and justified from within by a spiritual attachment to the period. Undoubtedly, the tide of recent Italian history cannot be reversed. Thus, the war is felt to be not an interlude but the end of an era. In one sense Italy is only three years old. But other effects could have resulted from the same cause. What is a ceaseless source of wonder, ensuring the Italian cinema a wide moral audience among the Western nations, is the significance it gives to the portrayal of actuality. In a world already once again obsessed by terror and hate, in which reality is scarely any longer favored for its own sake but rather is rejected or excluded as a political symbol, the Italian cinema is certainly the only one which preserves, in the midst of the period it depicts, a revolutionary humanism.

Love and Rejection of Reality

The recent Italian films are at least prerevolutionary. They all reject implicitly or explicitly, with humor, satire or poetry, the reality they are using, but they know better, no matter how clear the stand taken, than to treat this reality as a medium or a means to an end. To condemn it does not of necessity mean to be in bad faith. They never forget that the world *is,* quite simply, before it is something to be condemned. It is silly and perhaps as naïve as Beaumarchais' praise of the tears induced by melodrama. But does one not, when coming out of an Italian film, feel better, an urge to change the order of things, preferably by persuading people, at least those who can be persuaded, whom only blindness, prejudice, or ill-fortune had led to harm their fellow men?

That is why, when one reads resumés of them, the scenarios of many Italian films are open to ridicule. Reduced to their plots, they are often just moralizing melodramas, but on the screen everybody in the film is overwhelmingly real. Nobody is reduced to the condition of an object or a symbol that would allow one to hate them in comfort without having first to leap the hurdle of their humanity.

I am prepared to see the fundamental humanism of the current Italian films as their chief merit.* They offer an opportunity to savor, before the

---

* I do not hide from myself the astute political role more or less consciously concealed under this communicative generosity. It could happen that tomorrow the priest in *Roma Città Aperta* and the Communist former member of the Resistance might not get on so well. It could happen that the Italian cinema might soon become political and partisan. There might be a few half-lies hidden somewhere in all this. The cleverly pro-American *Paisà* was shot by Christian Democrats and Communists. But it is not being a dupe, it is simply being sensible to accept in a work what is in it. At the moment the Italian cinema is more sociological than political. By that I mean that such concrete social realities as poverty,

time finally runs out on us, a revolutionary flavor in which terror has yet no part.

An Amalgam of Players

What naturally first struck the public was the high quality of the acting. *Roma Città Aperta* enriched the world's screen with a performer of the first order, Anna Magnani the unforgettable pregnant young woman, Fabrizzi the priest, Pagliero a member of the Resistance, and others whose performances rival in retrospect the most stirring of film characterizations in the past. Reports and news items in the public press naturally made a point of letting us know that *Sciuscà* was filled with genuine street urchins, that Rossellini shot crowds taken at random at the scene of the action, that the heroine of the first story of *Paisà* was an illiterate girl discovered on the dockside. As for Anna Magnani, admittedly she was a professional but from the world of the *café-concert*. Maria Michi, well, she was just a little girl who worked in a movie house.

Although this type of casting is unusual in films, it is not new. On the contrary, its continual use, by various realistic schools ever since the days of Lumière, shows it to be a true law of the cinema, which the Italian

the black market, the administration, prostitution and unemployment do not seem to have given place in the public conscience to the *a priori* values of politics. Italian films rarely tell us the political party of the director or whom he is intending to flatter. This state of affairs derives doubtless from ethnic temperament, but it also derives from the political situation in Italy and what is customary in the Communist party on that peninsula.

Political associations apart, this revolutionary humanism has its source likewise in a certain consideration for the individual; the masses are but rarely considered to be a positive social force. When they are mentioned it is usually in order to demonstrate their destructive and negative character *vis-à-vis* the heroes: the theme of the man in the crowd. From this point of view the two latest important Italian films, *Caccia tragica* and *Il sole sorge ancora,* are significant exceptions, indicating perhaps a new trend.

The director De Santis who worked very closely with Vergano as his assistant on *Il sole sorge ancora* is the only one ever to take a group of men, a collective, as the protagonist of a drama.

school simply confirms and allows us to formulate with conviction. In the old days of the Russian cinema too, we admired its preference for nonprofessional actors who played on the screen the roles of their daily lives. Actually, a legend has grown up around the Russian films. The theater had a strong influence on certain Soviet schools and although the early films of Eisenstein had no actors, as realist a film as *The Road to Life* was in fact played by professionals from the theater and ever since then the actors in Soviet films have continued to be professionals, just as they have in other countries.

No major cinematographic school between 1925 and the present Italian cinema can boast of the absence of actors, but from time to time a film outside the ordinary run will remind us of the advantage of not using them. Such a film will always be specifically only slightly removed from a social document. Take two examples: *L'Espoir* and *La Dernière Chance*. Around them, too, a legend has grown up. The heroes in the Malraux film are not all part-time actors called on for the moment to play their day-to-day selves. It is true that some of them are, but not the principal characters. The peasant, for example, was a well-known Madrid comic actor. As regards *La Dernière Chance,* the Allied soldiers were actually airmen shot down over Switzerland, but the Jewish woman was a stage actress. Only productions like *Tabu* are entirely without professional actors, but here, as in children's films, we are dealing with a special genre in which a professional actor would be almost unthinkable. More recently, Rouquier in *Farrebique* set out to play the game to the hilt. While noting his success, let us also note that it is practically unique and that the problems presented by a peasant film, so far as the acting is concerned, are no different from those of an exotic film. So far from being an example to be followed, *Farrebique* is a special case in no way invalidating the law that I propose to call the law of the amalgam. It is not the absence of professional actors that is, historically, the hallmark of social realism nor of the Italian film. Rather, it is specifically the rejection of the star concept and the casual mixing of professionals and of those who just act occasionally. It is important to avoid casting the professional in the role for which he is known. The public should not be burdened with any preconceptions. It is significant that the peasant in *Espoir* was a theater comedian, Anna Magnani a singer of popular songs, and Fabrizzi a music-hall clown. That someone is an actor does not mean he must not be used. Quite the opposite. But his professionalism should be called into service only insofar as it allows him to be more flexible in his response to the requirements of the *mise en scène,* and to have a better grasp of the character. The nonprofessionals are naturally chosen for their suitability for the part, either because they fit it physically or because there is some parallel between the role and their lives. When the amalgamation comes off—but experience shows that it will not unless some "moral" requirements are met in the script—the result is precisely that extraordinary feeling of truth that one gets from the current Italian films. Their faithfulness to a script which stirs them deeply and which calls for the minimum of theatrical pretense sets up a kind of osmosis among the cast. The technical inexperience of the amateur is helped out by the experience of the professionals while the professionals themselves benefit from the general atmosphere of authenticity.

However, if a method so beneficent to the art of the cinema has only been employed here and there, it is because unfortunately it contains within itself the seeds of its own destruction. The chemical balance of the amalgam is of necessity unstable, and nothing can prevent it evolving to the point at which it reintroduces the aesthetic dilemma it originally solved—that between the enslavement of the star and the documentary without actors. This disintegration can be observed most clearly and quickly in children's films or films using native peoples. Little Rari of *Tabu,* they say, ended up as a prostitute in Poland, and we all know what happens to children raised to stardom by their first film. At best they turn out to be infant actor prodigies, but that is something else again. Indispensable as are the factors of inexperience and naïveté, obviously they cannot survive repetition. One cannot envisage the Farrebique family appearing in half a dozen films and finally being signed up by Hollywood. As for the professionals who are not stars, the process of disintegration operates a little differently. The public is to blame. While an accepted star is received everywhere as himself, the success of a film is apt to identify the ordinary actor with the role he plays in it. Producers are only too glad to repeat a success by catering to the well-known public fondness for seeing their favorite actors in their established roles. And even if an actor has sense enough to avoid being confined to a single role, it is still a fact that his face and some recurring mannerisms in his acting having become familiar will prevent the amalgam with nonprofessionals from taking place.

Aestheticism, Realism and Reality

Faithfulness to everyday life in the scenario, truth to his part in an actor, however, are simply the basic materials of the aesthetic of the Italian film.

One must beware of contrasting aesthetic refinement and a certain crudeness, a certain instant effectiveness of a realism which is satisfied just to present reality. In my view, one merit of the Italian film will be that it has demonstrated that every realism in art was first profoundly aesthetic. One always felt it was so, but in the reverberations of the accusations of witchcraft that some people today are making against actors suspected of a pact with the demon of art for art's sake, one has tended to forget it. The real like the imaginary in art is the concern of the artist alone. The flesh and blood of reality are no easier to capture in the net of literature or cinema than are gratuitous flights of the imagination. Or to put it another way, even when inventions and complexity of forms are no longer being applied to the actual content of the work, they do not cease thereby to have an influence on the effectiveness of the means. Because the Soviet cinema was too forgetful of this, it slipped in twenty years from first to last place among the great film-producing nations. *Potemkin* turned the cinema world upside down not just because of its political message, not even because it replaced the studio plaster sets with real settings and the star with an anoynmous crowd, but because Eistenstein was the greatest montage theoretician of his day, because he worked with Tissé, the finest camerman of his day, and because Russia was the focal point of cinematographic thought—in short, because the "realist" films Russia turned out secreted more aesthetic know-how than all the sets and performances and lighting and artistic interpretation of the artiest works of German expressionism.

It is the same today with the Italian cinema. There is nothing aesthetically retrogressive about its neorealism, on the contrary, there is progress in expression, a triumphant evolution of the language of cinema, an extension of its stylistics.

Let us first take a good look at the cinema to see where it stands today. Since the expressionist heresy came to an end, particularly after the arrival of sound, one may take it that the general trend of cinema has been toward realism. Let us agree, by and large, that film sought to give the spectator as perfect an illusion of reality as possible within the limits of the logical demands of cinematographic narrative and of the current limits of technique. Thus the cinema stands in contrast to poetry, painting, and theater, and comes ever closer to the novel. It is not my intention here to justify this basic aesthetic trend of modern cinema, be it on technical, psychological, or economic grounds. I simply state it for this once without thereby prejudging either the intrinsic validity of such an evolution or the extent to which it is final.

But realism in art can only be achieved in one way—through artifice.

Every form of aesthetic must necessarily choose between what is worth preserving and what should be discarded, and what should not even be considered. But when this aesthetic aims in essence at creating the illusion of reality, as does the cinema, this choice sets up a fundamental contradiction which is at once unacceptable and necessary: necessary because art can only exist when such a choice is made. Without it, supposing total cinema was here and now technically-possible, we would go back purely to reality. Unacceptable because it would be done definitely at the expense of that reality which the cinema proposes to restore integrally. That is why it would be absurd to resist every new technical development aiming to add to the realism of cinema, namely sound, color, and stereoscopy. Actually the "art" of cinema lives off this contradiction. It gets the most out of the potential for abstraction and symbolism provided by the present limits of the screen, but this utilization of the residue of conventions abandoned by technique can work either to the advantage or to the detriment of realism. It can magnify or neutralize the effectiveness of the elements of reality that the camera captures. One might group, if not classify in order of importance, the various styles of cinematography in terms of the added measure of reality. We would define as "realist," then, all narrative means tending to bring an added measure of reality to the screen. Reality is not to be taken quantitatively. The same event, the same object, can be represented in various ways. Each representation discards or retains various of the qualities that permit us to recognize the object on the screen. Each introduces, for didactic or aesthetic reasons, abstractions that operate more or less corrosively and thus do not permit the original to subsist in its entirety. At the conclusion of this inevitable and necessary "chemical" action, for the initial reality there has been substituted an illusion of reality composed of a complex of abstraction (black and white, plane surface), of conventions (the rules of montage, for example), and of authentic reality. It is a necessary illusion but it quickly induces a loss of awareness of the reality itself, which becomes identified in the mind of the spectator with its cinematographic representation. As for the film maker, the moment he has secured this unwitting complicity of the public, he is increasingly tempted to ignore reality. From habit and laziness he reaches the point when he himself is no longer able to tell where lies begin or end. There could never be any question of calling him a liar because his art consists in lying. He is just no longer in control of his art. He is its dupe, and hence he is held back from any further conquest of reality.

From *Citizen Kane* to *Farrebique*

Recent years have brought a noticeable evolution of the aesthetic of cinema in the direction of realism. The two most significant events in this evolution in the history of the cinema since 1940 are *Citizen Kane* and *Paisà*. Both mark a decisive step forward in the direction of realism but by different paths. If I bring up the film of Orson Welles before I analyze the

27

stylistics of the Italian film, it is because it will allow us to place the latter in its true perspective. Orson Welles restored to cinematographic illusion a fundamental quality of reality—its continuity. Classical editing, deriving from Griffith, separated reality into successive shots which were just a series of either logical or subjective points of view of an event. A man locked in a cell is waiting for the arrival of his executioner. His anguished eyes are on the door. At the moment the executioner is about to enter we can be quite sure that the director will cut to a close shot of the door handle as it slowly turns. This close-up is justified psychologically by the victim's concentration on the symbol of his extreme distress. It is this ordering of the shots, this conventional analysis of the reality continuum, that truly goes to make up the cinematographic language of the period.

The construction thus introduces an obviously abstract element into reality. Because we are so used to such abstractions, we no longer sense them. Orson Welles started a revolution by systematically employing a depth of focus that had so far not been used. Whereas the camera lens, classically, had focused successively on different parts of the scene, the camera of Orson Welles takes in with equal sharpness the whole field of vision contained simultaneously within the dramatic field. It is no longer the editing that selects what we see, thus giving it an *a priori* significance, it is the mind of the spectator which is forced to discern, as in a sort of parallelepiped of reality with the screen as its cross-section, the dramatic spectrum proper to the scene. It is therefore to an intelligent use of a specific step forward that *Citizen Kane* owes its realism. Thanks to the depth of focus of the lens, Orson Welles restored to reality its visible continuity.

We clearly see with what elements of reality the cinema has enriched itself. But from other points of view, it is also evident that it has moved away from reality or at least that it gets no nearer to it than does the classical aesthetic. In ruling out, because of the complexity of his techniques, all recourse to nature in the raw, natural settings,* exteriors, sun-

---

* Matters become complicated when we are dealing with urban settings. Here the Italians are at an undoubted advantage. The Italian city, ancient or modern, is prodigiously photogenic. From antiquity, Italian city planning has

light, and nonprofessional actors, Orson Welles rejects those qualities of the authentic document for which there is no substitute and which, being likewise a part of reality, can themselves establish a form of realism. Let us contrast *Citizen Kane* and *Farrebique*—in the latter, a systematic determination to exclude everything that was not primarily natural material is precisely the reason why Rouquier failed in the area of technical perfection.

Thus, the most realistic of the arts shares the common lot. It cannot make reality entirely its own because reality must inevitably elude it at some point. Undoubtedly an improved technique, skillfully applied, may narrow the holes of the net, but one is compelled to choose between one kind of reality and another. The sensitiveness resembles the sensitiveness of the retina. The nerve endings that register color and intensity of light are not at all the same, the density of one being ordinarily in inverse ratio to that of the other. Animals that have no difficulty in making out the shape of their quarry in the dark are almost color blind.

Between the contrasting but equally pure kinds of realism represented by *Farrebique* on the one hand and *Citizen Kane* on the other, there is a wide variety of possible combinations. For the rest, the margin of loss of the real, implicit in any realist choice, frequently allows the artist, by the use of any aesthetic convention he may introduce into the area thus left vacant, to increase the effectiveness of his chosen form of reality. Indeed we have a remarkable example of this in the recent Italian cinema. In the absence of technical equipment, the Italian directors have been obliged to record the sound and dialogue after the actual filming. The net

---

remained theatrical and decorative. City life is a spectacle, a *commedia dell'arte* that the Italians stage for their own pleasure. And even in the poorest quarters of the town, the coral-like groupings of the houses, thanks to the terraces and balconies, offer outstanding possibilities for spectacle. The courtyard is an Elizabethan set in which the show is seen from below, the spectators in the gallery being the actors in the comedy. A poetic documentary was shown at Venice consisting entirely of an assemblage of shots of courtyards. What more can you say when the theatrical façades of the palazzi combine their operatic effects with the stage-like architecture of the houses of the poor? Add to this the sunshine and the absence of clouds (chief enemy of shooting on exteriors) and you have explained why the urban exteriors of Italian films are superior to all others.

result is a loss of realism. However, left free to use the camera unfettered by the microphone, such directors have thereby profited by the occasion to enlarge the camera's field of action and its mobility with, consequently, an immediate raising of the reality coefficient.

Future technical improvments which will permit the conquest of the properties of the real (color and stereoscopy for example) can only increase the distance between the two realist poles which today are situated in the area surrounding *Farrebique* and *Citizen Kane.* The quality of the interior shots will in fact increasingly depend on a complex, delicate and cumbersome apparatus. Some measure of reality must always be sacrificed in the effort of achieving it.

Paisà

How do you fit the Italian film into the realist spectrum? After trying to trace the geographical boundaries of this cinema, so penetrating in its portrayal of the social setting, so meticulous and perceptive in its choice of authentic and significant detail, it now remains for us to fathom its aesthetic geology.

We would clearly be deluding ourselves if we pretended to reduce recent Italian production to certain common, easily definable characteristics applicable to all directors. We will simply try to single out those characteristics with the widest application, reserving the right when the occasion arises to limit our concern to the most significant films. Since we must also make a choice, we will arrange, by implication, the major Italian films in concentric circles of decreasing interest around *Paisà,* since it is this film of Rossellini's that yields the most aesthetic secrets.

Narrative Technique

As in the novel, the aesthetic implicit in the cinema reveals itself in its narrative technique. A film is always presented as a succession of fragments of imaged reality on a rectangular surface of given proportions, the ordering of the images and their duration on the screen determining its import.

The objective nature of the modern novel, by reducing the strictly grammatical aspect of its stylistics to a minimum, has laid bare the secret essence of style.* Certain qualities of the language of Faulkner, Hemingway, or Malraux would certainly not come through in translation, but the essential quality of their styles would not suffer because their style is almost completely identical with their narrative technique—the ordering in time of fragments of reality. The style becomes the inner dynamic principle of the narrative, somewhat like the relation of energy to matter or the specific physics of the work, as it were. This it is which distributes the fragmented realities across the aesthetic spectrum of the narrative, which polarizes the filings of the facts without changing their chemical composition. A Faulkner, a Malraux, a Dos Passos, each has his personal universe which is defined by the nature of the facts reported, but also by the law of gravity which holds them suspended above chaos. It will be useful, therefore, to arrive at a definition of the Italian style on the basis of the scenario, of its genesis, and of the forms of exposition that it follows. Unfortunately the demon of melodrama that Italian film makers seem incapable of exorcising takes over every so often, thus imposing a dramatic necessity on strictly foreseeable events. But that is another story. What matters is the creative surge, the special way in which the situations are brought to life. The necessity inherent in the narrative is biological rather than dramatic. It burgeons and grows with all the verisimilitude of life.† One must not con-

---

* In Camus' *L'Etranger,* for example, Sartre has clearly demonstrated the link between the author's metaphysic and the repeated use of the passé composé, a tense of singular modal poverty.

† Nearly all the credits of an Italian film list under the heading "scenario" a good dozen names. This imposing evidence of collaboration need not be taken too seriously. It is intended to provide the producers with a naïvely political assurance. It usually consists of one Christian Democrat and one Communist (just as in the film there is a Marxist and a priest); the third screenwriter has a reputation for story construction; the fourth is a gag man; the fifth because he is a good dialogue writer; the sixth because he has a fine feeling for life. The result is no better or no worse than if there had been only one screen writer, but the Italian

clude that this method, on the face of it, is less aesthetic than a slow and meticulous preplanning. But the old prejudice that time, money, and resources have a value of their own is so rooted that people forget to relate them to the work and to the artist. Van Gogh repainted the same picture ten times, very quickly, while Cézanne would return to a painting time and again over the years. Certain genres call for speed, for work done in the heat of the moment, but surgery could not call for a greater sureness of touch, for greater precision. It is only at this price that the Italian film has that air of documentary, a naturalness nearer to the spoken than to the written account, to the sketch rather than to the painting. It calls for the ease and sure eye of Rossellini, Lattuada, Vergano, and de Santis. In their hands the camera is endowed with well-defined cinematographic tact, wonderfully sentitive antennae which allow them with one stroke to get precisely what they are after. In *Il Bandito,* the prisoner, returning from Germany, finds his house in ruins. Where a solid building once stood there is now just a pile of stones surrounded by broken-down walls. The camera shows us the man's face. Then, following the movement of his eyes, it travels through a 360-degree turn which gives us the whole spectacle. This panning shot is doubly original. First, because at the outset, we stand off from the actor since we are looking at him by way of a camera trick, but during the traveling shot we become identified with him to the point of feeling surprised when, the 360-degree pan having been completed, we return to his face with its expression of utter horror. Second, because the speed of this subjective panning shot varies. It starts with a long slide, then it comes almost to a halt, slowly studies the burned and shattered walls with the same rhythm of the man's watching eye, as if directly impelled by his concentration.

I have had to dwell at some length on this minor example to avoid making a purely abstract affirmation concerning what I regard, in an almost psychological sense of the word, as cinematic "tact." A shot of this

---

notion of a scenario fits in with their concept of a collective paternity according to which everyone contributes an idea without any obligation on the part of the director to use it. Rather than the assembly line of American screenwriters, this interdependence of improvisation is like that of *commedia dell'arte* or jazz.

kind by virtue of its dynamism belongs with the movement of a hand drawing a sketch, leaving a space here, filling in there, here sketching round the subject, and there bringing it into relief. I am thinking of the slow motion in the documentary on Matisse which allows us to observe, beneath the continuous and uniform arabesques of the stroke, the varying hesitations of the artist's hand. In such a case the camera movement is important. The camera must be equally as ready to move as to remain still. Traveling and panning shots do not have the same god-like character that the Hollywood camera crane has bestowed on them. Everything is shot from eye-level or from a concrete point of view, such as a roof top or window. Technically speaking, all the memorable poetry of the children's ride on the white horse in *Sciuscià* can be attributed to a low-level camera angle which gives the riders on their mounts the appearance of an equestrian statue. In *Sortilège,* Christian Jacques went to a great deal more trouble over his phantom horse. But all that cinematic virtuosity did not prevent his animal from having the prosaic look of a broken-down cab horse. The Italian camera retains something of the human quality of the Bell and Howell newsreel camera, a projection of hand and eye, almost a living part of the operator, instantly in tune with his awareness.

As for the photography, the lighting plays only a minor expressive role. First, because lighting calls for a studio, and the greater part of the filming is done on exteriors or in real-life settings. Second, because documentary camera work is identified in our minds with the grey tones of newsreels. It would be a contradiction to take any great pains with or to touch up excessively the plastic quality of the style.

As we have thus far attempted to describe it, the style of Italian films would appear to belong with a greater or less degree of skill and mastery of technique or feeling to the same family as quasi-literary journalism, to an ingenious art, pleasing, lively, and even moving, but basically a minor art. This is sometimes true even though one may actually rank the genre fairly high in the aesthetic hierarchy. It would be unjust and untrue to see such an assessment as the final measure of this particular technique. Just as, in literature, reportage with its ethic of objectivity (perhaps it would be more correct to say with its ethic of seeming objectivity) has simply provided a basis for a new aesthetic of the novel, so the technique of the Italian film makers results in the best films especially in *Paisà,* with its aesthetic of narrative that is both complex and original.*

Paisà is unquestionably the first film to resemble closely a collection of short stories. Up to now we had only known the film composed of sketches —a bastard and phony type of film if ever there was one. Rossellini tells us, in succession, six stories of the Italian Liberation. This historical element is the only thing they have in common. Three of them, the first, the fourth, and the last, are taken from the Resistance. The others are droll or pathetic or tragic episodes occurring on the fringes of the Allied advance. Prostitution, the black market, and a Franciscan convent alike provide the story material. There is no progression other than a chronological ordering of the story beginning with the landing of an Allied force in Sicily. But their social, historical, and human foundation gives them a unity enough to constitute a collection perfectly homogeneous in its diversity. Above all, the length of each story, its form, contents, and aesthetic duration gives us for the first time precisely the impression of a short story. The Naples episode of the urchin—a black-market expert, selling the clothes of a drunk Negro soldier—is an excellent Saroyan story. Another makes us think of Hemingway, yet another (the first) of Faulkner. I am not merely referring to the tone or the subject, but in a profound way to the style. Unfortunately one cannot put a film sequence in quotation marks like a paragraph, and hence any literary description of one must of necessity be incomplete. However, here is an episode from the final story which reminds me now of Hemingway, now of Faulkner:

1. A small group of Italian partisans and Allied soldiers have been given a supply of food by a family of fisher folk living in an isolated farmhouse in the heart of the marshlands of the Po delta. Having been handed

---

* I will not at this point get into an historical argument over the origins or the foreshadowing of the "novel of reportage" in the nineteenth century. Besides, the novels of Stendhal or the naturalists were concerned with frankness, acuteness, and perspicacity of observation, rather than with objectivity properly so called. Facts for their own sake had not yet acquired that kind of ontological autonomy, which makes of them a succession of sealed off monads, strictly limited by their appearance.

a basket of eels, they take off. Some while later, a German patrol discovers this, and executes the inhabitants of the farm. 2. An American officer and a partisan are wandering at twilight in the marshes. There is a burst of gunfire in the distance. From a highly elliptical conversation we gather that the Germans have shot the fishermen. 3. The dead bodies of the men and women lie stretched out in front of the little farmhouse. In the twilight, a half-naked baby cries endlessly.

Even with such a succinct description, this fragment of the story reveals enormous ellipses—or rather, great holes. A complex train of action is reduced to three or four brief fragments, in themselves already elliptical enough in comparison with the reality they are unfolding. Let us pass over the first purely descriptive fragment. The second event is conveyed to us by something only the partisans can know—distant gunfire. The third is presented to us independently of the presence of the partisans. It is not even certain that there were any witnesses to the scene. A baby cries besides its dead parents. There is a fact. How did the Germans discover that the parents were guilty? How is it that the child is still alive? That is not the film's concern, and yet a whole train of connected events led to this particular outcome. In any case, the film maker does not ordinarily show us everything. That is impossible—but the things he selects and the things he leaves out tend to form a logical pattern by way of which the mind passes easily from cause to effect. The technique of Rossellini undoubtedly maintains an intelligible succession of events, but these do not mesh like a chain with the sprockets of a wheel. The mind has to leap from one event to the other as one leaps from stone to stone in crossing a river. It may happen that one's foot hesitates between two rocks, or that one misses one's footing and slips. The mind does likewise. Actually it is not of the essence of a stone to allow people to cross rivers without wetting their feet any more than the divisions of a melon exist to allow the head of the family to divide it equally. Facts are facts, our imagination makes use of them, but they do not exist inherently for this purpose. In the usual shooting script (according to a process resembling the classical novel form) the fact comes under the scrutiny of the camera, is divided up, analyzed, and put together again, undoubtedly without entirely losing its factual nature; but the latter, presumably, is enveloped in abstraction, as the clay of a brick is enveloped by the wall which is not as yet present but which will multiply its parallelepipeds. For Rossellini, facts take on a meaning, but not like a tool whose function has predetermined its form. The facts follow one another, and the mind is forced to observe their resemblance; and thus, by recalling one another, they end by meaning something which was inherent in each and which is, so to speak, the moral of the story—a moral the mind cannot fail to grasp since it was drawn from reality itself. In the Florentine episode, a woman crosses the city while it is still occupied by a number of Germans and groups of Italian Fascists; she is on her way to meet her fiancé, a leader of the Italian underground, accompanied by a man who likewise is looking for his wife and child. The attention of the camera following them, step by step, though it will share all the difficulties they encounter, all their dangers, will however be impartially divided between the heroes of the adventure and the conditions they must encounter. Actually, everything that is happening in a Florence in the throes of the Liberation is of a like importance. The personal adventures of the two individuals blend into the mass of other adventures, just as one attempts to elbow one's way into a crowd to recover something one has lost. In the course of making one's way one sees in the eyes of those who stand aside the reflections of other concerns, other passions, other dangers alongside which one's own may well be merely laughable. Ultimately and by chance, the woman learns, from a wounded partisan, that the man she is looking for is dead. But the statement from which she learned the news was not aimed straight at her—but hit her like a stray bullet. The impeccable line followed by this recital owes nothing to classical forms that are standard for a story of this kind Attention is never artificially focused on the heroine. The camera makes no pretense at being psychologically subjective. We share all the more fully in the feelings of the protagonists because it is easy for us to sense what they are feeling; and also because the pathetic aspect of the episode does not derive from the fact that a woman has lost the man she loves but from the special place this drama holds among a thousand others, apart from and yet also part of the complete drama of the Liberation of Florence. The camera, as if making an impartial report, confines itself to following a woman searching for a man, leaving to us the task of being alone with her, of understanding her, and of sharing her suffering.

In the admirable final episode of the partisans surrounded in the marshlands, the muddy waters of the Po Delta, the reeds stretching away to the horizon, just sufficiently tall to hide the man crouching down in the little flat-bottomed boat, the lapping of the waves against the wood, all occupy a place of equal importance with the men. This dramatic role played by the marsh is due in great measure to deliberately intended qualities in the photography. This is why the horizon is always at the same height. Maintaining the same proportions between water and sky in every shot brings out one of the basic characteristics of this landscape. It is the exact equivalent, under conditions imposed by the screen, of the inner feeling men experience who are living between the sky and the water and whose lives are at the mercy of an infinitesimal shift of angle in relation to the horizon. This shows how much subtlety of expression can be got on exteriors from a camera in the hands of the man who photographed *Paisà*.

The unit of cinematic narrative in *Paisà* is not the "shot," an abstract view of a reality which is being analyzed, but the "fact." A fragment of concrete reality in itself multiple and full of ambiguity, whose meaning emerges only after the fact, thanks to other imposed facts between which the mind establishes certain relationships. Unquestionably, the director chose these "facts" carefully while at the same time respecting their factual integrity. The closeup of the door knob referred to earlier was less a fact than a sign brought into arbitrary relief by the camera, and no more independent semantically than a preposition in a sentence. The opposite is true of the marsh or the death of the peasants.

But the nature of the "image facts" is not only to maintain with the other image facts the relationships invented by the mind. These are in a sense the centrifugal properties of the images—those which make the narrative possible. Each image being on its own just a fragment of reality existing before any meanings, the entire surface of the scene should manifest an equally concrete density. Once again we have here the opposite of the "door-knob" type of scene, in which the color of the enamel, the dirt marks at the level of the hand, the shine of the metal, the worn-away look are just so many useless facts, concrete parasites of an abstraction fittingly dispensed with.

In *Paisà* (and I repeat that I imply by this, in varying degrees, all Italian films) the closeup of the door knob would be replaced, without any loss of that peculiar quality of which it is part, by the "image fact" of a door whose concrete characteristics would be equally visible. For the same reason the actors will take care never to dissociate their performance from the decor or from the performance of their fellow actors. Man himself is just one fact among others, to whom no pride of place should be given *a priori*. That is why the Italian film makers alone know how to shoot successful scenes in buses, trucks, or trains, namely because these scenes combine to create a special density within the framework of which they know how to portray an action without separating it from its material context and without loss of that uniquely human quality of which it is an integral part. The subtlety and suppleness of movement within these cluttered spaces, the naturalness of the behavior of everyone in the shooting area, make of these scenes supreme bravura moments of the Italian cinema.

The Realism of the Italian Cinema and the Technique of the American Novel

The absence of any film documentation may have operated against a clear understanding of what I have so far written. I have arrived at the point of characterizing as similar the styles of Rossellini in *Paisà* and of Orson Welles in *Citizen Kane*. By diametrically opposite technical routes each arrives at a scenario with roughly the same approach to reality— the depth of focus of Welles and the predisposition toward reality of Rossellini. In both we find the same dependence of the actor relative to the setting, the same realistic acting demanded of everyone in the scene whatever their dramatic importance. Better still, although the styles are so different, the narrative follows basically the same pattern in *Citizen Kane* and in *Paisà*.

In short, although they use independent techniques, without the least possibility of a direct influence one on the other, and possessed of temperaments that could hardly be less compatible, Rossellini and Welles have, to all intents and purposes, the same basic aesthetic objective, the same aesthetic concept of realism.

I had leisure enough as I watched the film to compare the narrative of *Paisà* with that of some modern novelists and short story writers. Besides, the resemblances between the technique of Orson Welles and that of the American novel, notably Dos Passos, are sufficiently obvious to allow me now to expound my thesis. The aesthetic of the Italian cinema, at least in its most elaborate manifestations and in the work of a director as conscious of his medium as Rossellini, is simply the equivalent on film of the American novel.

Let us clearly understand that we are here concerned with something quite other than banal adaptation. Hollywood, in fact, never stops adapting American novels for the screen. We are familiar with what Sam Wood did to *For Whom the Bell Tolls*. Basically all he wanted was to retell a plot. Even if he had been faithful to the original, sentence by sentence, he would not, properly speaking, have transferred anything from the book to the screen. The films that have managed to translate something of the style of novels into images can be counted on the fingers of one hand, by which I mean the very fabric of the narrative, the law of gravity that governs the ordering of the facts, in Faulkner, Hemingway, and Dos Passos. We had to wait for Orson Welles to show what the cinema of the American novel would be.*

So then, while Hollywood adapts bestseller after bestseller at the same

---

* The cinema nevertheless has come close to these truths on several occasions, in the case of Feuillade for example, or of Stroheim. More recently, Malraux has clearly understood the parallel between a certain style of novel and film narrative. Finally, instinctively and by virtue of his genius, Renoir had already applied in *La Règle du jeu* the essentials of the principles of depth of focus and the simultaneous presentation of all the actors in a scene. He had explained this in a prophetic article in 1938 in the review *Point*.

time moving further away from the spirit of this literature, it is in Italy, naturally and with an ease that excludes any notion of deliberate and willful imitation, that the cinema of American literature has become a reality. Unquestionably we must not underestimate the popularity of the American novelists in Italy, where their works were translated and assimilated long before they were in France, and the influence for example of Saroyan on Vittorini is common knowledge. I would sooner cite, in preference to these dubious cause-and-effect relations, the exceptional affinity of the two civilizations as revealed by the Allied occupation. The G.I. felt himself at home at once in Italy, and the *paisan* was at once on familiar terms with the G.I., black or white. The widespread black market and the presence everywhere of prostitution, wherever the American army went, is by no means the least convincing example of the symbiosis of two civilizations. It is not for nothing that American soldiers are important characters in most recent Italian films; and that they are much at home there speaks volumes.

Although some paths have been opened by literature and the occupation, the phenomenon cannot be explained on this level alone. American films are being made in Italy today but never has the Italian film been at the same time more typically Italian. The body of references I have adopted has excluded similarities even less disputable, for example the Italian "tale," the *commedia dell'arte* and the technique of the fresco. Rather than an influence one on the other, it is an accord between cinema and literature, based on the same profound aesthetic data, on the same concept of the relation between art and reality. It is a long while since the modern novel created its realist revolution, since it combined behavorism, a reporter's technique, and the ethic of violence. Far from the cinema having the slightest effect on this evolution, as is commonly held today, a film like *Paisà* proves that the cinema was twenty years behind the contemporary novel. It is not the least of the merits of the Italian cinema that it has been able to find the truly cinematic equivalent for the most important literary revolution of our time.

LA TERRA TREMA

THE SUBJECT MATTER of *La Terra Trema* owes nothing to the war: it deals with an attempted revolt by the fishermen of a small Sicilian village against the economic stranglehold exerted by the local fleet-owning fish merchants. I might define it as a kind of super-*Farrebique* about fishermen. The parallels with Rouquier's film are many: first, its quasidocumentary realism; then (if one may so put it) the exoticism intrinsic to the subject matter; and, too, the underlying "human geography" (for the Sicilian family, the hope of freeing themselves from the merchants amounts to the same thing as the installation of electricity for the Farrebique family). Although in *La Terra Trema,* a Communist film, the whole village is involved, the story is told in terms of a single family, ranging from grandfather to grandchildren. This family was as much out of its element in the sumptuous reception Universalia gave in its honor at the Excelsior in Venice as the Farrebique family had been at its press party in Paris. Visconti, like Rouquier, did not want to use professional actors, not even Rossellini's kind of "amalgam." His fishermen are fishermen in real life. He recruited them on the scene of his story's action—if that is the proper term here, for here (as in *Farrebique)* the action deliberately resists the seductions of "drama": the story unfolds without regard for the rules of suspense, its only resources a concern with things themselves, as in life. But with these negative rather than positive aspects of the story the resemblances to *Farrebique* end; *La Terra Trema* is as remote as could be in style from *Farrebique*.

Visconti, like Rouquier, aimed at and unquestionably achieved a paradoxical synthesis of realism and aestheticism but the poetry of *Farrebique* is due, in essence, to montage—for example, the winter and spring sequences. To obtain this synthesis in his film, Visconti has not had recourse to the effects one can produce from the juxtaposition of images. Each image here contains a meaning of its own which it expresses fully. This is the reason why it is difficult to see more than a tenuous relation between *La Terra Trema* and the Soviet cinema of the second half of the twenties, to which montage was essential. We may add now that it is not by means of symbolism in the imagery either that meaning manifests itself here—I mean, the symbolism to which Eisenstein and Rouquier resort. The aesthetic peculiar to the image here is always plastic; it avoids any inclination to the epic. As staggeringly beautiful as the fishing fleet may be when it leaves the harbor, it is still just the village fleet, not, as in *Potemkin*, the Enthusiasm and the Support of the people of Odessa who send out the fishing boats loaded with food for the rebels.

But, one may ask, where is art to take refuge if the realism one is proposing is so ascetic? Everywhere else. In the quality of the photography, especially. Our compatriot Aldo, who before his work on this film did nothing of real note and was known only as a studio cameraman, has here created a profoundly original style of image, unequaled anywhere (as far as I know) but in the short films which are being made in Sweden by Arne Sucksdorff.

To keep my explanations brief, I will only note that, in an article on Italian film of 1946, "Le réalisme cinématographique et l'école italienne de la liberation" (*Esprit,* January, 1948), I had examined some aspects of the kind of film realism then current, and that I was led to see *Farrebique* and *Citizen Kane* as the two poles of realistic technique. The realism of *Farrebique* derives from the object itself, of *Citizen Kane* from the way it structures what it represents. In *Farrebique* everything is real. In *Kane* everything has been reconstructed in a studio—but only because such depth of field and such rigorously composed images could not be obtained on location. *Paisà* stands somewhere between the two but closer to *Farrebique* for its images, while the realistic aesthetic works it way into the film between the component blocs of reality through its peculiar conception of narrative.

The images of *La Terra Trema* achieve what is at once a paradox and *tour de force* in integrating the aesthetic realism of *Citizen Kane* with the documentary realism of *Farrebique*. If this is not, strictly speaking, the first time depth of focus has been used outside the studio, it is at least the first time it has been used as consciously and as systematically as it is here out of doors, in the rain and even in the dead of night, as well as indoors in the real-life settings of the fishermen's homes. I cannot linger over the technical *tour de force* which this represents, but I would like to emphasize that depth of focus has naturally led Visconti (as it led Welles) not only to reject montage but, in some literal sense, to invent a new kind of shooting script.* His "shots" (if one is justified in retaining the term) are unusually long—some lasting three or four minutes. In each, as one might expect, several actions are going on simultaneously. Visconti also seems to have wanted, in some systematic sense, to base the construction of his image on the event itself. If a fisherman rolls a cigarette, he spares us nothing: we see the whole operation; it will not be reduced to its dramatic or symbolic meaning, as is usual with montage. The shots are often fixed-frame, so people and things may enter the frame and take up position; but Visconti is also in the habit of using a special kind of panning shot which moves very slowly over a very wide arc: this is the only camera movement which he allows himself, for he excludes all tracking shots and, of course, every unusual camera angle.

The unlikely sobriety of this structure is possible only because of the remarkable plastic balance maintained—a balance which only a photograph could absolutely render here. But above and beyond the merits of its purely formal properties, the image reveals an intimate knowledge of the subject matter on the part of the film makers. This is especially re-

---

* For a note on Bazin's use of technical terms, see p. 181.

markable in the interiors, which hitherto have eluded film. The difficulties attendant on lighting and shooting make it almost impossible to use real interiors as settings. It has been done occasionally, but the results from an aesthetic point of view have been far inferior to what can be achieved on exteriors. Here, for the first time throughout an entire film there was no variation in quality between interior and exterior as to the style of the shooting script, the performance of the actors, and the results of the photography. Visconti is worthy of the novelty of his triumph. Despite the poverty—or even because of the simple "ordinariness" of this household of fishermen, an extraordinary kind of poetry, at once intimate and social, emanates from it.

The masterly way in which Visconti has handled his actors deserves the highest praise. This is by no means the first time in history of film that nonprofessional actors have been used, but never before (except perhaps in "exotic" films, where the problem is somewhat specialized) have the actors been so skillfully integrated with the most specifically aesthetic elements of the film. Rouquier never knew how to handle his family without our being conscious of a camera. The embarrassment, the repressed laughter, the awkwardness are skillfully covered up by the editing which always cuts just in the nick of time. In *La Terra Trema,* the actor, sometimes on camera for several minutes at a time, speaks, moves, and acts with complete naturalness—one might even say, with unimaginable grace. Visconti is from the theater. He has known how to communicate to the nonprofessionals of *La Terra Trema* something more than naturalness, namely that stylization of gesture that is the crowning achievement of an actor's profession. If festival juries were not what they are, the Venice festival prize for best acting should have gone to the fishermen of *La Terra Trema.*

Visconti lets us sees that the Italian neorealism of 1946 has been left far behind on more than one score. Hierarchies in art are fairly pointless, but cinema is too young an art still, too involved in its own evolution to be able to indulge in repeating itself for any length of time. Five years in cinema is the equivalent of an entire literary generation. It is the merit of Visconti to have managed a dialectical integration of the achievements of recent Italian film with a larger, richer aesthetic for which the term "realism" has not too much meaning now. I am not saying that *La Terra Trema* is superior to *Paisà* or to *La Caccia tragica* but only that it does, at least, have the merit of having left them behind from an historical standpoint. Seeing the best Italian films of 1948, I had the impression that Italian cinema was doomed to repeat itself to its utter exhaustion.

La Terra Trema is the only original way out of the aesthetic impasse, and in that sense, one might suppose, it bears the burden of our hopes.

Does this mean that those hopes will be fulfilled? No, unhappily, it is not certain, for *La Terra Trema* runs counter, still, to some filmic principles with which Visconti will have in future films to deal somewhat more convincingly than he does here. In particular, his disinclination to sacrifice anything to drama has one obvious and serious consequence: *La Terra Trema* bores the public. A film with a limited action, it lasts longer than three hours. If you add that the language used in the film is a dialectal Sicilian (which, given the photographic style of the image, it is impossible to subtitle), and that not even Italians understand it, you can see that this is somewhat austere "entertainment" and faces no more than a restricted commercial future. I am sincere when I say that I hope Universalia will play the Maecenas sufficiently to enable Visconti, while himself sharing the cost from his large personal fortune, to finish the trilogy he projects of which *La Terra Trema* is only the first part. We will then, at best, have some filmic monster, whose highly social and political preoccupations will nonetheless remain inaccessible to the general public. In the world of cinema, it is not necessary that everyone approve every film, provided that what prompts the public's incomprehension can be compensated for by the other things. In other words, the aesthetic of *La Terra Trema* must be applicable to dramatic ends if it is to be of service in the evolution of cinema.

One has to take into account too—and this is even more disturbing, in view of what one has the right to expect from Visconti himself—a dangerous inclination to aestheticism. This great aristocrat, an artist to the tips of his fingers, is a Communist, too—do I dare say a synthetic one?

La Terra Trema lacks inner fire. One is reminded of the great Renaissance painters who, without having to do violence to themselves, were able to paint such fine religious frescoes in spite of their deep indifference to Christinianity. I am not passing judgment on the sincerity of Visconti's communism. But what is sincerity? Obviously, at issue is not some paternalistic feeling for the proletariat. Paternalism is a bourgeois phenomenon, and Visconti is an aristocrat. What is at issue is, maybe, an aesthetic participation in history. Whatever it be, though, we are a long way off from the telling conviction of *Potemkin* or *The End of Saint Petersburg* or even (the theme is even the same) of *Piscator*. There is no doubt that the film does have propaganda value, but this value is purely objective: there is no moving eloquence to bolster its documentary vigor. This is how Visconti intended it to be. This decision is not in itself unattractive. But it involves him in a fairly risky bet, which he may not necessarily be able to cover, at least in terms of film. Let us hope that his future work will show us that it can. As it stands, however, it will not, unless it can avoid falling in the direction in which it is already leaning perilously.

BICYCLE THIEF

WHAT SEEMS to me most astonishing about the Italian cinema is that it appears to feel it should escape from the aesthetic impasse to which neo-realism is said to have led. The dazzling effects of 1946 and 1947 having faded away, one could reasonably fear that this useful and intelligent re-action against the Italian aesthetic of the superspectacle and, for that matter, more generally, against the technical aestheticism from which cinema suffered all over the world, would never get beyond an interest in a kind of superdocumentary, or romanticized reportage. One began to realize that the success of *Roma Città Aperta, Paisà,* or *Sciuscià* was inseparable from a special conjunction of historical circumstances that took its meaning from the Liberation, and that the technique of the films was in some way magnified by the revolutionary value of the subject. Just as some books by Malraux or Hemingway find in a crystallization of journalistic style the best narrative form for a tragedy of current events, so the films of Rossellini or De Sica owed the fact that they were major works, masterpieces, simply to a fortuitous combination of form and subject matter. But when the novelty and above all the flavor of their technical crudity have exhausted their surprise effect, what remains of Italian "neorealism" when by force of circumstances it must revert to traditional subjects: crime stories, psychological dramas, social cus-toms? The camera in the street we can still accept, but doesn't that admirable nonprofessional acting stand self-condemned in proportion as its discoveries swell the ranks of international stars? And, by way of generalizing about this aesthetic pessimism: "realism" can only occupy in art a dialectical position—it is more a reaction than a truth. It remains then to make it part of the aesthetic it came into existence to verify. In any case, the Italians were not the last to downgrade their "neorealism." I think there is not a single Italian director, including the most neorealist, who does not insist that they must get away from it.

French critics too feel themselves a prey to scruples—especially since this vaunted neorealism early showed signs of running out of steam. Comedies, agreeable enough in themselves, appeared on the scene to exploit with visible ease the formula of *Quattro passi fra le nuvole* or *Vivere in Pace*. But worst of all was the emergence of a neorealist superspectacle in which the search for real settings, action taken from everyday life, portrayals of lower-class mileux, "social" backgrounds, became an academic stereotype far more detestable than the elephants of *Scipio Africanus*. For a neorealist film may have every defect except that of being academic. Thus at Venice *Il Patto col diavolo* by Luigi Chiarini, a somber melodrama of rural love, took visible pains to find a contemporary alibi in a story of conflict between shepherds and woodsmen. Although well done on some accounts, *In nome della legge,* which the Italians tried to push to the fore at Knokke-le-Zoute, cannot escape similar criticisms. One will notice incidentally, from these two examples, that neorealism is now preoccupied with rural problems, perhaps prudently in view of the fate of urban neorealism. The closed-in countryside has replaced the open city.

However that may be, the hopes that we placed in the new Italian school had started to turn into uneasiness, or even skepticism, all the more since the aesthetic of neorealism forbids it to repeat itself or plagiarize itself in the way that is possible and even normal in some traditional genres (the crime film, the western, the atmospheric film, and so on). Already we were beginning to look toward England whose recent cinematic rebirth is likewise, in part, the fruit of realism: that of the school of documentarists who, before and during the war, had gone deeply into the resources offered by social and technical realities. A film like *Brief Encounter* would probably have been impossible without the ten years of preparation by Grierson, Cavalcanti, or Rotha. But the English, instead of breaking with the technique and the history of European and American cinema, have succeeded in combining a highly refined aestheticism with the advances of a certain realism. Nothing could be more tightly structured, more carefully prepared, than *Brief Encounter*—nothing less conceivable without the most up-to-date studio resources, without clever and established actors; yet can we imagine a more realistic portrait of English manners and psychology? Certainly, David Lean has gained nothing by making over, this year, a kind of second *Brief Encounter: The Passionate Friends,* presented at the Cannes festival. But it is against repetition of the subject matter that one can reasonably protest, not against the repetition of the techniques, which could be used over and over indefinitely.*

Have I played devil's advocate long enough? For let me now make a confession: my doubts about the Italian cinema have never gone so far, but all the arguments I have invoked have been used by intelligent men— especially in Italy—nor are they unfortunately without some semblance of validity. They have also often troubled me, and I subscribe to some of them.

On the other hand there is a film called *Ladri di Biciclette* and two other films that I hope we will soon get to know in France. With *Ladri di Biciclette* De Sica has managed to escape from the impasse, to reaffirm anew the entire aesthetic of neorealism.

Ladri di Biciclette certainly *is* neorealist, by all the principles one can deduce from the best Italian films since 1946. The story is from the lower classes, almost populist: an incident in the daily life of a worker. But the film shows no extraordinary events such as those which befall the fated workers in Gabin films. There are no crimes of passion, none of those

---

* This paragraph, which redounds to the glory of the English cinema but not that of the writer, has been retained to bear witness to critical illusions about English cinema which I was not the only one to entertain. *Brief Encounter* made almost as great an impression as *Roma Città Aperta.* Time has shown which of the two had a real cinematic future. Besides, the Noël Coward-David Lean film owed very little to the Grierson school of documentary. [Note by Bazin some time after the article was written, probably in 1956.—TR.]

grandiose coincidences common in detective stories which simply transfer to a realm of proletarian exoticism the great tragic debates once reserved for the dwellers on Olympus. Truly an insignificant, even a banal incident: a workman spends a whole day looking in vain in the streets of Rome for the bicycle someone has stolen from him. This bicycle has been the tool of his trade, and if he doesn't find it he will again be unemployed. Late in the day, after hours of fruitless wandering, he too tries to steal a bicycle. Apprehended and then released, he is as poor as ever, but now he feels the shame of having sunk to the level of the thief.

Plainly there is not enough material here even for a news item: the whole story would not deserve two lines in a stray-dog column. One must take care not to confuse it with realist tragedy in the Prévert or James Cain manner, where the initial news item is a diabolic trap placed by the gods amid the cobble stones of the street. In itself the event contains no proper dramatic valence. It takes on meaning only because of the social (and not psychological or aesthetic) position of the victim. Without the haunting specter of unemployment, which places the event in the Italian society of 1948, it would be an utterly banal misadventure. Likewise, the choice of a bicycle as the key object in the drama is characteristic both of Italian urban life and of a period when mechanical means of transportation were still rare and expensive. There is no need to insist on the hundreds of other meaningful details that multiply the vital links between the scenario and actuality, situating the event in political and social history, in a given place at a given time.

The techniques employed in the *mise en scène* likewise meet the most exacting specifications of Italian neorealism. Not one scene shot in a studio. Everything was filmed in the streets. As for the actors, none had the slightest experience in theater or film. The workman came from the Breda factory, the child was found hanging around in the street, the wife was a journalist.

These then are the facts of the case. It is clear that they do not appear to recall in any sense the neorealism of *Quattro passi fra le nuvole, Vivere in Pace,* or *Sciuscià.* On the face of it then one should have special reasons for being wary. The sordid side of the tale tends toward that most debatable aspect of Italian stories: indulgence in the wretched, a systematic search for squalid detail.

If *Ladri di Biciclette* is a true masterpiece, comparable in rigor to *Paisà,* it is for certain precise reasons, none of which emerge either from a simple outline of the scenario or from a superficial disquisition on the technique of the *mise en scène.*

The scenario is diabolically clever in its construction; beginning with the alibi of a current event it makes good use of a number of systems of dramatic coordinates radiating in all directions. *Ladri di Biciclette* is certainly the only valid Communist film of the whole past decade precisely because it still has meaning even when you have abstracted its social significance. Its social message is not detached, it remains immanent in the event, but it is so clear that nobody can overlook it, still less take exception to it, since it is never made explicitly a message. The thesis implied is wondrously and outrageously simple: in the world where this workman lives, the poor must steal from each other in order to survive. But this thesis is never stated as such, it is just that events are so linked together that they have the appearance of a formal truth while retaining an anecdotal quality. Basically, the workman might have found his bicycle in the middle of the film; only then there would have been no film. (Sorry to have bothered you, the director might say; we really did think he would never find it, but since he has, all is well, good for him, the performance is over, you can turn up the lights.) In other words, a propaganda film would try to prove that the workman could not find his bicycle, and that he is inevitably trapped in the vicious circle of poverty. De Sica limits himself to showing that the workman cannot find his bicycle and that as a result he doubtless will be unemployed again. No one can fail to see that it is the accidental nature of the script that gives the thesis its quality of necessity; the slightest doubt cast on the necessity of the events in the scenario of a propaganda film renders the argument hypothetical.

Although on the basis of the workman's misfortune we have no alternative but to condemn a certain kind of relation between a man and his work, the film never makes the events or the people part of an economic or political Manicheism. It takes care not to cheat on reality, not only by

51

contriving to give the succession of events the appearance of an accidental and as it were anecdotal chronology but in treating each of them according to its phenomenological integrity. In the middle of the chase the little boy suddenly needs to piss. So he does. A downpour forces the father and son to shelter in a carriageway, so like them we have to forego the chase and wait till the storm is over. The events are not necessarily signs of something, of a truth of which we are to be convinced, they all carry their own weight, their complete uniqueness, that ambiguity that characterizes any fact. So, if you do not have the eyes to see, you are free to attribute what happens to bad luck or to chance. The same applies to the people in the film. The worker is just as deprived and isolated among his fellow trade unionists as he is walking along the street or even in that ineffable scene of the Catholic "Quakers" into whose company he will shortly stray, because the trade union does not exist to find lost bikes but to transform a world in which losing his bike condemns a man to poverty. Nor does the worker come to lodge a complaint with the trade union but to find comrades who will be able to help him discover the stolen object. So here you have a collection of proletarian members of a union who behave no differently from a group of paternalistic bourgeois toward an unfortunate workman. In his private misfortune, the poster hanger is just as alone in his union as in church (buddies apart that is—but then who your buddies are is your own affair). But this parallel is extremely useful because it points up a striking contrast. The indifference of the trade union is normal and justified because a trade union is striving for justice not for charity. But the cumbersome paternalism of the Catholic "Quakers" is unbearable, because their eyes are closed to his personal tragedy while they in fact actually do nothing to change the world that is the cause of it. On this score the most successful scene is that in the storm under the porch when a flock of Austrian seminarians crowd around the worker and his son. We have no valid reason to blame them for chattering so much and still less for talking German. But it would be difficult to create a more *objectively* anticlerical scene.

Clearly, and I could find twenty more examples: events and people are never introduced in support of a social thesis—but the thesis emerges fully armed and all the more irrefutable because it is presented to us as something thrown in into the bargain. It is our intelligence that discerns and shapes it, not the film. De Sica wins every play on the board without ever having made a bet.

This technique is not entirely new in Italian films and we have elsewhere stressed its value at length both apropos of *Paisà* and of *Allemania Anno Zero,* but these two films were based on themes from either the Resistance or the war. *Ladri di Biciclette* is the first decisive example of the possibility of the conversion of this kind of objectivity to other, similar subjects. De Sica and Zavattini have transferred neorealism from the Resistance to the Revolution.

Thus the thesis of the film is hidden behind an objective social reality which in turn moves into the background of the moral and psychological drama which could of itself justify the film. The idea of the boy is a stroke of genius, and one does not know definitely whether it came from the script or in the process of directing, so little does this distinction mean here any more. It is the child who gives to the workman's adventure its ethical dimension and fashions, from an individual moral standpoint, a drama that might well have been only social. Remove the boy, and the story remains much the same. The proof: a *resumé* of it would not differ in detail. In fact, the boy's part is confined to trotting along beside his father. But he is the intimate witness of the tragedy, its private chorus. It is supremely clever to have virtually eliminated the role of the wife in order to give flesh and blood to the private character of the tragedy in the person of the child. The complicity between father and son is so subtle that it reaches down to the foundations of the moral life. It is the admiration the child feels for his father and the father's awareness of it which gives its tragic stature to the ending. The public shame of the worker, exposed and clouted in the open street, is of little account compared with the fact that his son witnessed it. When he feels tempted to steal the bike, the silent presence of the little child, who guesses what his father is thinking, is cruel to the verge of obscenity. Trying to get rid of him by sending him to take the streetcar is like telling a child in some cramped apartment to go and wait on the landing outside for an hour. Only in the best Chaplin films are there situations of an equally overwhelming conciseness.

In this connection, the final gesture of the little boy in giving his hand to his father has been frequently misinterpreted. It would be unworthy of the film to see here a concession to the feelings of the audience. If De Sica gives them this satisfaction it is because it is a logical part of the drama. This experience marks henceforth a definite stage in the relations between father and son, rather like reaching puberty. Up to that moment the man has been like a god to his son; their relations come under the heading of admiration. By his action the father has now compromised them. The tears they shed as they walk side by side, arms swinging, signify their despair over a paradise lost. But the son returns to a father who has fallen from grace. He will love him henceforth as a human being, shame and all. The hand that slips into his is neither a symbol of forgiveness nor of a childish act of consolation. It is rather the most solemn gesture that could ever mark the relations between a father and his son: one that makes them equals.

It would take too long to enumerate the multiple secondary functions of the boy in the film, both as to the story structure and as to the *mise en scène* itself. However, one should at least pay attention to the change of tone (almost in the musical sense of the term) that his presence introduces into the middle of the film. As we slowly wander back and forth between the little boy and the workman we are taken from the social and economic plane to that of their private lives, and the supposed death by drowning of the child, in making the father suddenly realize the relative insignificance of his misfortune, creates a dramatic oasis (the restaurant scene) at the heart of the story. It is, however, an illusory one, because the reality of this intimate happiness in the long run depends on the precious bike. Thus the child provides a dramatic reserve which, as the occasion arises, serves as a counterpoint, as an accompaniment, or moves on the contrary into the foreground of the melodic structure. This function in the story is, furthermore, clearly observable in the orchestration of the steps of the child and of the grownup. Before choosing this particular child, De Sica did not ask him to perform, just to walk. He wanted to play off the striding gait of the man against the short trotting steps of the child, the harmony of this discord being for him of capital importance for the understanding of the film as a whole. It would be no exaggeration to say that *Ladri di Biciclette* is the story of a walk through Rome by a father and his son. Whether the child is ahead, behind, alongside—or when, sulking after having had his ears boxed, he is dawdling behind in a gesture of revenge—what he is doing is never without meaning. On the contrary, it is the phenomenology of the script.

It is difficult, after the success of this pairing of a workman and his son, to imagine De Sica having recourse to established actors. The absence of professional actors is nothing new. But here again *Ladri di Biciclette* goes further than previous films. Henceforth the cinematic purity of the actors does not derive from skill, luck, or a happy combination of a subject, a period, and a people. Probably too much importance has been attached to the ethnic factor. Admittedly the Italians, like the Russians, are the most naturally theatrical of people. In Italy any little street urchin is the equal of a Jackie Coogan and life is a perpetual *commedia dell'arte*. However, it seems to me unlikely that these acting talents are shared equally by the Milanese, the Neapolitans, the peasants of the Po, or the fishermen of Sicily. Racial difference apart, the contrasts in their history, language, and economic and social condition would suffice to cast doubt on a thesis that sought to attribute the natural acting ability of the Italian people simply to an ethnic quality. It is inconceivable that films as different as *Paisà, Ladri di Biciclette, La Terra Trema,* and even *Il Cielo sulla Palude* could share in common such a superbly high level of acting. One could conceive that the urban Italian has a special gift for spontaneous histrionics, but the peasants in *Cielo sulla Palude* are absolute cavemen beside the farmers of *Farrebique*. Merely to recall Rouquier's film in connection with Genina's is enough at least in this respect to relegate the experiment of the French director to the level of a touchingly patronizing effort. Half the dialogue in *Farrebique* is spoken off-stage because Rouquier could never get the peasants not to laugh during a speech of any length. Genina in *Cielo sulla Palude,* Visconti in *La Terra Trema,* both handling peasants or fishermen by the dozen, gave them complicated roles and got them to recite long speeches in scenes in which the camera concentrated on their faces as pitilessly as in an American studio. It is an understatement to say that these temporary actors are good or even perfect. In these films the very concept of actor, performance, character has no longer any meaning. An actorless cinema? Undoubtedly. But the original meaning of the formula is now outdated, and we should talk today of a cinema without acting, of a cinema of which we no longer ask whether the character gives a good performance or not, since here man and the character he portrays are so completely one.

We have not strayed as far as it might seem from *Ladri di Biciclette*. De Sica hunted for his cast for a long time and selected them for specific characteristics. Natural nobility, that purity of countenance and bearing that the common people have . . . He hesitated for months between this person and that, took a hundred tests only to decide finally, in a flash and by intuition on the basis of a silhouette suddenly come upon at the bend of a road. But there is nothing miraculous about that. It is not the unique excellence of this workman and this child that guarantees the quality of their performance, but the whole aesthetic scheme into which they are fitted. When De Sica was looking for a producer to finance his film, he finally found one, but on condition that the workman was played by Cary Grant. The mere statement of the problem in these terms shows the absurdity of it. Actually, Cary Grant plays this kind of part extremely well, but it is obvious that the question here is not one of playing of a part but of getting away from the very notion of doing any such thing. The worker had to be at once as perfect and as anonymous and as objective as his bicycle.

This concept of the actor is no less "artistic" than the other. The performance of this workman implies as many gifts of body and of mind and as much capacity to take direction as any established actor has at his command. Hitherto films that have been made either totally or in part without actors, such as *Tabú, Thunder over Mexico, Mother,* have seemingly been successes that are either out of the ordinary or limited to a certain genre. There is nothing on the other hand, unless it be sound prudence, to prevent De Sica from making fifty films like *Ladri di Biciclette*. From now on we know that the absence of professional actors in no way limits the choice of subject. The film without names has finally established its own aesthetic existence. This in no sense means that the cinema of the future will no longer use actors: De Sica who is one of the world's finest actors would be the first to deny this. All it means is that some subjects handled in a certain style can no longer be made with professional actors and that the Italian cinema has definitely imposed these working conditions, just as naturally as it imposed authentic settings. It is this transition from an admirable *tour de force,* precarious as this may be, into an exact and infallible technique that marks a decisive stage in the growth of Italian neorealism.

With the disappearance of the concept of the actor into a transparency seemingly as natural as life itself, comes the disappearance of the set. Let us understand one another, however. De Sica's film took a long time to prepare, and everything was as minutely planned as for a studio superproduction, which as a matter of fact, allows for last-minute improvisations, but I cannot remember a single shot in which a dramatic effect is born of the shooting script properly so called, which seems as neutral as in a Chaplin film. All the same, the numbering and titling of shots does not noticeably distinguish *Ladri di Biciclette* from any ordinary film. But their selection has been made with a view to raising the limpidity of the event to a maximum, while keeping the index of refraction from the style to a minimum.

This objectivity is rather different from Rossellini's in *Paisà* but it belongs to the same school of aesthetics. One may criticize it on the same grounds that Gide and Martin du Garde criticized romantic prose—that it must tend in the direction of the most neutral kind of transparency. Just as the disappearance of the actor is the result of transcending a style of performance, the disappearance of the *mise en scène* is likewise the fruit of a dialectical progress in the style of the narrative. If the event is sufficient unto itself without the direction having to shed any further light on it by means of camera angles, purposely chosen camera positions, it is because it has reached that stage of perfect luminosity which makes it possible for an art to unmask a nature which in the end resembles it. That is why the impression made on us by *Ladri di Biciclette* is unfailingly that of truth.

If this supreme naturalness, the sense of events observed haphazardly as the hours roll by, is the result of an ever-present although invisible system of aesthetics, it is definitely the prior conception of the scenario which allows this to happen. Disappearance of the actor, disappearance of *mise en scène?* Unquestionably, but because the very principle of *Ladri di Biciclette* is the disappearance of a story.

The term is equivocal. I know of course that there is a story but of a different kind from those we ordinarily see on the screen. This is even the reason why De Sica could not find a producer to back him. When Roger Leenhardt in a prophetic critical statement asked years ago "if the cinema is a spectacle," he was contrasting the dramatic cinema with the novel-like structure of the cinematic narrative. The former borrows from the theater its hidden springs. Its plot, conceived as it may be specifically for the screen, is still the alibi for an action identical in essence with the action of the classical theater. On this score the film is a spectacle like a play. But on the other hand, because of its realism and the equal treatment it gives to man and to nature the cinema is related, aesthetically speaking, to the novel.

Without going too far into a theory of the novel—a debatable subject —let us say that the narrative form of the novel or that which derives from it differs by and large from the theater in the primacy given to events over action, to succession over causality, to mind over will. The conjunction belonging to the theater is "therefore," the particle belonging to the novel is "then." This scandalously rough definition is correct to the extent that it characterizes the two different movements of the mind in thinking, namely that of the reader and that of the onlooker. Proust can lose us in a madeleine, but a playwright fails in his task if every reply does not link our interest to the reply that is to follow. That is why a novel may be laid down and then picked up again. A play cannot be cut into pieces. The total unity of a spectacle is of its essence. To the extent that it can realize the physical requirements of a spectacle, the cinema cannot apparently escape the spectacle's pyschological laws, but it has also at its disposal all the resources of the novel. For that reason, doubtless, the cinema is congenitally a hybrid. It conceals a contradiction. Besides, clearly, the progression of the cinema is toward increasing its novel-like potential. Not that we are against filmed theater, but if the screen can in some conditions develop and give a new dimension to the theater, it is of necessity at the expense of certain scenic values—the first of which is the physical presence of the actor. Contrariwise, the novel at least ideally need surrender nothing to the cinema. One may think of the film as a supernovel of which the written form is a feeble and provisional version.

This much briefly said, how much of it can be found in the present condition of the cinematographic spectacle? It is impossible to overlook the spectacular and theatrical needs demanded of the screen. What remains to be decided is how to reconcile the contradiction.

The Italian cinema of today is the first anywhere in the world to have enough courage to cast aside the imperatives of the spectacular. *La Terra Trema* and *Cielo sulla Palude* are films without "action," in the unfolding of which, somewhat after the style of the epic novel, no concession is made to dramatic tension. Things happen in them each at its appointed hour, one after the other, but each carries an equal weight. If some are fuller of meaning than others, it is only in retrospect. We are free to use either "therefore" or "then." *La Terra Trema,* especially, is a film destined to be virtually a commercial failure, unexploitable without cuts that would leave it unrecognizable.

That is the virtue of De Sica and Zavattini. Their *Ladri di Biciclette* is solidly structured in the mold of a tragedy. There is not one frame that is not charged with an intense dramatic power, yet there is not one either which we cannot fail to find interesting, its dramatic continuity apart.

The film unfolds on the level of pure accident: the rain, the seminarians, the Catholic Quakers, the restaurant—all these are seemingly interchangable, no one seems to have arranged them in order on a dramatic spectrum. The scene in the thieves' quarter is significant. We are not sure that the man who was chased by the workman is actually the bicycle thief, and we shall never know if the epileptic fit was a pretense or genuine. As an "action" this episode would be meaningless had not its novel-like interest, its value as a fact, given it a dramatic meaning to boot.

It is in fact on its reverse side, and by parallels, that the action is assembled—less in terms of "tension" than of a "summation" of the events. Yes, it *is* a spectacle, and what a spectacle! *Ladri di Biciclette,* however, does not depend on the mathematical elements of drama, the action does not exist beforehand as if it were an "essence." It follows from the pre-existence of the narrative, it is the "integral" of reality. De Sica's supreme achievement, which others have so far only approached with a varying degree of success or failure, is to have succeeded in discovering the cinematographic dialectic capable of transcending the contradiction between the action of a "spectacle" and of an event. For this reason, *Ladri di Biciclette* is one of the first examples of pure cinema. No more actors, no more story, no more sets, which is to say that in the perfect aesthetic illusion of reality there is no more cinema.

DE SICA: METTEUR EN SCÈNE

I MUST confess to the reader that my pen is paralyzed by scruples because of the many compelling reasons why I should not be the one to introduce De Sica to him.

First, there is the presumption implied in a Frenchman wanting to teach Italians something about their own cinema in general,* and, in particular, about the man who is possibly their greatest director. Besides, when I imprudently accepted the honor of introducing De Sica in these pages, I was particularly conscious of my admiration for *Ladri di Biciclette* and I had not yet seen *Miracolo a Milano*. We in France have of course, seen *Ladri di Biciclette, Sciuscia,* and *I Bambini ci guardano,* but lovely as *Sciuscià* is, and revealing as it is of the talents of De Sica, it bears, side by side with certain sublime discoveries, traces of the apprentice director. The scenario occasionally succumbs to melodramatic indulgence, and the direction has a certain poetic elegance, a lyrical quality, that today it seems to me De Sica is concerned to avoid. In short, we do not have there as yet the personal style of the director. His complete and final mastery is

---

* This article, dating from 1952, was originally published in Italian by Edizione Guanda (Parma, 1953). The text in the French edition of *Qu'est-ce que le cinéma?*, from which this is translated, was itself a translation of the Italian text.

revealed in *Ladri di Biciclette* to such an extent that the film seems to include all the efforts that went into the making of its predecessors.

But can one judge a director by a single film? This film is sufficient proof of the genius of De Sica, but not of the future forms that this genius will take. As an actor, De Sica is no newcomer to the cinema, but one must still call him "young" as a director—a director of the future. In spite of the resemblances we will observe between them, *Miracolo a Milano* differs greatly in inspiration and structure from *Ladri di Biciclette*. What will his next film be? Will it reveal trends that appear only of minor importance in the previous works? In short, we are undertaking to speak of the style of a director of the first order on the basis of just two films—one of which seems to conflict with the orientation of the other. This is all right if one does not confuse the role of a critic with that of a prophet. I have no trouble explaining why I admire *Ladri* and *Miracolo* but that is something very different from pretending to deduce from these two films what are the permanent and definitive characteristics of their maker's talent.

All the same we would willingly have done that for Rossellini after *Roma Città Aperta* and *Paisà*. What we would have been able to say (and what we actually wrote in France) ran the risk of being modified by Rossellini's subsequent films, but not of being given the lie. The style of Rossellini belongs to a different aesthetic family. The rules of its aesthetics are plain to see. It fits a vision of the world directly adapted to a framework of *mise en scène*. Rossellini's style is a way of seeing, while de Sica's is primarily a way of feeling. The *mise en scène* of the former lays siege to its object from outside. I do not mean without understanding and feeling—but that this exterior approach offers us an essential ethical and metaphysical aspect of our relations with the world. In order to understand this statement one need only compare the treatment of the child in *Allemania Anno Zero* and in *Sciuscià* and *Ladri di Biciclette*.

Rossellini's love for his characters envelops them in a desperate awareness of man's inability to communicate; De Sica's love, on the contrary, radiates from the people themselves. They are what they are, but lit from within by the tenderness he feels for them. It follows that Rossellini's direction comes between his material and us, not as an artificial obstacle set up between the two, but as an unbridgeable, ontological distance, a congenital weakness of the human being which expresses itself aesthetically in terms of space, in forms, in the structure of his *mise-en-soène*. Because we are aware of it as a lack, a refusal, an escape from things, and hence finally as a kind of pain, it follows that it is easier for us to be aware of it, easier for us to reduce it to a formal method. Rossellini cannot alter this without himself passing through a personal moral revolution.

By contrast, De Sica is one of those directors whose sole purpose seems to be to interpret their scenarios faithfully, whose entire talent derives from the love they have for their subject, from their ultimate understanding of it. The *mise-en-scène* seems to take shape after the fashion of a natural form in living matter. Despite a different kind of sensibility and a marked concern for form, Jacques Feyder in France also belongs to this family of directors whose one method of work seems to be to treat their subject honestly. This neutrality is illusory but its apparent existence does not make the critic's task any easier. It divides up the output of the film maker into so many special cases that, given one more film, all that has preceded it might be called into question. It is a temptation therefore to see only craftsmanship where one is looking for style, the generous humility of a clever technician meeting the demands of the subject instead of the creative imprint of a true *auteur*.

The *mise-en-scène* of a Rossellini film can be readily deduced from the images he uses, whereas De Sica forces us to arrive at his *mise-en-scène* inductively from a visual narrative which does not seem to admit of it.

Finally and above all, the case of De Sica is up to now inseparable from his collaboration with Zavattini, even more than is that of Marcel Carné in France with Jacques Prévert. There is no more perfect example in the history of the cinema of a symbiosis of screen writer and director. The fact that Zavattini collaborates with others, while Prévert has written few stories or scripts for anyone but Carné, makes no difference. On the contrary, what it allows us to conclude is that De Sica is the ideal director for Zavattini, the one who understands him best and most intimately. We have examples of the work of Zavattini without De Sica, but nothing of

De Sica without Zavattini. We are therefore undertaking arbitrarily to distinguish that which truly belongs to De Sica and all the more arbitrarily because we have just referred to his at least apparent humility in the face of the demands of the scenario.

We must likewise refuse to separate, as something against nature, what talent has so closely joined. May De Sica and Zavattini forgive us—and, in advance, the reader, who can have no interest in my scruples and who is waiting for me to get on with my task. I would like it understood, however, for my own peace of mind, that I aim only to attempt a few critical statements which the future will doubtless call into question; they are simply the personal testimony of a French critic writing in 1951 about work full of promise, the qualities of which are particularly resistant to aesthetic analysis. This profession of humility is in no sense just an oratorical precaution or a rhetorical formula. I beg the reader to believe that it is first and foremost the measure of my admiration.

It is by way of its poetry that the realism of De Sica takes on its meaning, for in art, at the source of all realism, there is an aesthetic paradox that must be resolved. The faithful reproduction of reality is not art. We are repeatedly told that it consists in selection and interpretation. That is why up to now the "realist" trends in cinema, as in other arts, consisted simply in introducing a greater measure of reality into the work: but this additional measure of reality was still only an effective way of serving an abstract purpose, whether dramatic, moral, or ideological. In France, "naturalism" goes hand in hand with the multiplication of novels and plays *à thèse*. The originality of Italian neorealism as compared with the chief schools of realism that preceded it and with the Soviet cinema, lies in never making reality the servant of some *à priori* point of view. Even the Dziga-Vertov theory of the "Kino-eye" only employed the crude reality of everyday events so as to give it a place on the dialectic spectrum of montage. From another point of view, theater (even realist theater) used reality in the service of dramatic and spectacular structure. Whether in the service of the interests of an ideological thesis, of a moral idea, or of a dramatic action, realism subordinates what it borrows from reality to its transcendent needs. Neorealism knows only immanence. It is from appearance only, the simple appearance of beings and of the world, that it knows how to deduce the ideas that it unearths. It is a phenomenology.

In the realm of means of expression, neorealism runs counter to the traditional categories of spectacle—above all, as regards acting. According to the classic understanding of this function, inherited from the theater, the actor expresses something: a feeling, a passion, a desire, an idea. From his attitude and his miming the spectator can read his face like an open book. In this perspective, it is agreed implicitly between spectator and actor that the same psychological causes produce the same physical effect and that one can without any ambiguity pass backwards and forwards from one to the other. This is, strictly speaking, what is called acting.

The structures of the *mise-en-scène* flow from it: decor, lighting, the angle and framing of the shots, will be more or less expressionistic in their relation to the behavior of the actor. They contribute for their part to confirm the meaning of the action. Finally, the breaking up of the scenes into shots and their assemblage is the equivalent of an expressionism in time, a reconstruction of the event according to an artificial and abstract duration: dramatic duration. There is not a single one of these commonly accepted assumptions of the film spectacle that is not challenged by neorealism.

First, the performance: it calls upon the actor to *be* before expressing himself. This requirement does not necessarily imply doing away with the professional actor but it normally tends to substitute the man in the street, chosen uniquely for his general comportment, his ignorance of theatrical technique being less a positively required condition than a guarantee against the expressionism of traditional acting. For De Sica, Bruno was a silhouette, a face, a way of walking.

Second, the setting and the photography: the natural setting is to the artificial set what the amateur actor is to the professional. It has, however, the effect of at least partly limiting the opportunity for plastic compositions available with artificial studio lighting.

But it is perhaps especially the structure of the narrative which is most radically turned upside down. It must now respect the actual duration of the event. The cuts that logic demands can only be, at best, descriptive. The assemblage of the film must never add anything to the existing reality. If it is part of the meaning of the film as with Rossellini, it is because the empty gaps, the white spaces, the parts of the event that we are not given, are themselves of a concrete nature: stones which are missing from the building. It is the same in life: we do not know everything that happens to others. Ellipsis in classic montage is an effect of style. In Rossellini's films it is a lacuna in reality, or rather in the knowledge we have of it, which is by its nature limited.

Thus, neorealism is more an ontological position than an aesthetic one. That is why the employment of its technical attributes like a recipe do not necessarily produce it, as the rapid decline of American neorealism proves. In Italy itself not all films without actors, based on a news item, and filmed in real exteriors, are better than the traditional melodramas and spectacles. On the contrary, a film like *Cronaca di un Amore* by Michelangelo Antonioni can be described as neorealist (in spite of the professional actors, of the detective-story-like arbitrariness of the plot, of expensive settings, and the baroque dress of the heroine) because the director has not relied on an expressionism outside the characters; he builds all his effects on their way of life, their way of crying, of walking, of laughing. They are caught in the maze of the plot like laboratory rats being sent through a labyrinth.

The diversity of styles among the best Italian directors might be advanced as a counter argument and I know how much they dislike the word neorealist. Zavattini is the only one who shamelessly admits to the title. The majority protest against the existence of a new Italian school of realism that would include them all. But that is a reflex reaction of the creator to the critic. The director as artist is more aware of his differences than his resemblances. The word neorealist was thrown like a fishing net over the postwar Italian cinema and each director on his own is doing his best to break the toils in which, it is claimed, he has been caught. However, in spite of this normal reaction, which has the added advantage of forcing us to review a perhaps too easy critical classification, I think there are good reasons for staying with it, even against the views of those most concerned.

Certainly the succinct definition I have just given of neorealism might appear on the surface to be given the lie by the work of Lattuada with its calculated, subtly architectural vision, or by the baroque exuberance, the romantic eloquence of De Santis, or by the refined theatrical sense of Visconti, who makes compositions of the most down-to-earth reality as if they were scenes from an opera or a classical tragedy. These terms are summary and debatable, but can serve for other possible epithets which consequently would confirm the existence of formal differences, of oppositions in style. These three directors are as different from one another as each is from De Sica, yet their common origin is evident if one takes a more general view and especially if one stops comparing them with one another and instead looks at the American, French, and Soviet cinema.

Neorealism does not necessarily exist in a pure state and one can conceive of it being combined with other aesthetic tendencies. Biologists distinguish, in genetics, characteristics derived from different parents, so-called dominant factors. It is the same with neorealism. The exacerbated theatricality of Malaparte's *Cristo Proibito* may owe a lot to German expressionism, but the film is nonetheless neorealist, radically different from the realist expressionism of a Fritz Lang.

But I seem to have strayed a long way from De Sica. This was simply that I might be better able to situate him in contemporary Italian production. The difficulty of taking a critical stand about the director of *Miracolo a Milano* might indeed be precisely the real indication of his style. Does not our inability to analyze its formal characteristics derive from the fact that it represents the purest form of neorealism, from the fact that *Ladri di Biciclette* is the ideal center around which gravitate, each in his own orbit, the works of the other great directors? It could be this very purity which makes it impossible to define, for it has as its paradoxical intention not to produce a spectacle which appears real, but rather to turn reality into a spectacle: a man is walking along the street and the onlooker is amazed at the beauty of the man walking.

Until further information is available, until the realization of Zavattini's dream of filming eighty minutes in the life of a man without a cut, *Ladri di Biciclette* is without a doubt the ultimate expression of neorealism.*

---

* Cf. note on *Umberto D* at the end of this chapter.

Though this *mise-en-scène* aims at negating itself, at being transparent to the reality it reveals, it would be naïve to conclude that it does not exist. Few films have been more carefully put together, more pondered over, more meticulously elaborated, but all this labor by De Sica tends to give the illusion of chance, to result in giving dramatic necessity the character of something contingent. Better still, he has succeeded in making dramatic contingency the very stuff of drama. Nothing happens in *Ladri di Biciclette* that might just as well not have happened. The worker could have chanced upon his bicycle in the middle of the film, the lights in the auditorium would have gone up and De Sica would have apologized for having disturbed us, but after all, we would be happy for the worker's sake. The marvelous aesthetic paradox of this film is that it has the relentless quality of tragedy while nothing happens in it except by chance. But it is precisely from the dialectical synthesis of contrary values, namely artistic order and the amorphous disorder of reality, that it derives its originality. There is not one image that is not charged with meaning, that does not drive home into the mind the sharp end of an unforgettable moral truth, and not one that to this end is false to the ontological ambiguity of reality. Not one gesture, not one incident, not a single object in the film is given a prior significance derived from the ideology of the director.

If they are set in order with an undeniable clarity on the spectrum of social tragedy, it is after the manner of the particles of iron filings on the spectrum of a magnet—that is to say, individually; but the result of this art in which nothing is necessary, where nothing has lost the fortuitous character of chance, is in effect to be doubly convincing and conclusive. For, after all, it is not surprising that the novelist, the playwright, or the film maker should make it possible for us to hit on this or that idea, since they put them there beforehand, and have seeded their work with them. Put salt into water, let the water evaporate in the fire of reflection, and you will get back the salt. But if you find salt in water drawn directly from a stream, it is because the water is salty by nature. The workman, Bruno, might have found his bike just as he might have won in the lottery—even poor people win lotteries. But this potential capacity only serves to bring out more forcefully the terrible powerlessness of the poor fellow. If he found his bike, then the enormous extent of his good luck would be an even greater condemnation of society, since it would make a priceless miracle, an exorbitant favor, out of the return to a human order, to a natural state of happiness, since it would signify his good fortune at not still being poor.

It is clear to what an extent this neorealism differs from the formal concept which consists of decking out a formal story with touches of reality. As for the technique, properly so called, *Ladri di Biciclette,* like a lot of other films, was shot in the street with nonprofessional actors but its true merit lies elsewhere: in not betraying the essence of things, in allowing them first of all to exist for their own sakes, freely; it is in loving them in their singular individuality. "My little sister reality," says De Sica, and she circles about him like the birds around Saint Francis. Others put her in a cage or teach her to talk, but De Sica talks with her and it is the true language of reality that we hear, the word that cannot be denied, that only love can utter.

To explain De Sica, we must go back to the source of his art, namely to his tenderness, his love. The quality shared in common by *Miracolo a Milano* and *Ladri di Biciclette,* in spite of differences more apparent than real, is De Sica's inexhaustible affection for his characters. It is significant then in *Miracolo a Milano,* that none of the bad people, even the proud or treacherous ones, are antipathetic. The junkyard Judas who sells his companions' hovels to the vulgar Mobbi does not stir the least anger in the onlookers. Rather would he amuse us in the tawdry costume of the "villain" of melodrama, which he wears awkwardly and clumsily: he is a good traitor. In the same way the new poor, who in their decline still retain the proud ways of their former fine neighborhoods, are simply a special variety of that human fauna and are not therefore excluded from the vagabond community—even if they charge people a lira a sunset. And a man must love the sunset with all his heart to come up with the idea of making people pay for the sight of it, and to suffer this market of dupes.

Besides, none of the principal characters in *Ladri di Biciclette* is unsympathetic. Not even the thief. When Bruno finally manages to get his hands on him, the public would be morally disposed to lynch him, as the crowd could have done earlier to Bruno. But the spark of genius in this film is to force us to swallow this hatred the moment it is born and to renounce judgment, just as Bruno will refuse to bring charges.

The only unsympathetic characters in *Miracolo a Milano* are Mobbi and his acolytes, but basically they do not exist. They are only conventional symbols. The moment De Sica shows them to us at slightly closer quarters, we almost feel a tender curiosity stirring inside us. "Poor rich people," we are tempted to say, "how deceived they are." There are many ways of loving, even including the way of the inquisitor. The ethics and politics of love are threatened by the worst heresies. From this point of view, hate is often more tender, but the affection De Sica feels for his creatures is no threat to them, there is nothing threatening or abusive about it. It is courtly and discreet gentleness, a liberal generosity, and it demands nothing in return. There is no admixture of pity in it even for the poorest or the most wretched, because pity does violence to the dignity of the man who is its object. It is a burden on his conscience.

The tenderness of De Sica is of a special kind and for this reason does not easily lend itself to any moral, religious, or political generalization. The ambiguities of *Miracolo a Milano* and *Ladri di Biciclette* have been used by the Christian Democrats and by the Communists. So much the better: a true parable should have something for everyone. I do not think De Sica and Zavattini were trying to argue anybody out of anything. I would not dream of saying that the kindness of De Sica is of greater value than the third theological virtue* or than class consciousness, but I see in the modesty of his position a definite artistic advantage. It is a guarantee of its authenticity while, at the same time, assuring it a universal quality. This penchant for love is less a moral question than one of personal and ethnic temperament. As for its authenticity, this can be explained in terms of a naturally happy disposition developed in a Neopolitan atmosphere. But these psychological roots reach down to deeper layers than the consciousness cultivated by partisan ideologies. Paradoxically and in virtue of their unique quality, of their inimitable flavor, since they have not been classi-

---

* The three theological virtues are faith, hope and charity.—TR.

fied in the categories of either morals or politics, they escape the latter's censure, and the Neopolitan charm of De Sica becomes, thanks to the cinema, the most sweeping message of love that our times have heard since Chaplin.

To anyone who doubted the importance of this, it is enough to point out how quick partisan critics were to lay claim to it. What party indeed could afford to leave love to the other? In our day there is no longer a place for unattached love but since each party can with equal plausibility lay claim to being the proprietor of it, it means that much authentic and naïve love scales the walls and penetrates the stronghold of ideologies and social theory.

Let us be thankful to Zavattini and De Sica for the ambiguity of their position—and let us take care not to see it as just intellectual astuteness in the land of Don Camillo, a completely negative concern to give pledges on all sides in return for an all-around censorship clearance. On the contrary it is a positive striving after poetry, the stratagem of a person in love, expressing himself in the metaphors of his time, while at the same time making sure to choose such of them as will open the hearts of everyone. The reason why there have been so many attempts to give a political exegesis to *Miracolo a Milano* is that Zavattini's social allegories are not the final examples of this symbolism, these symbols themselves being simply the allegory of love. Psychoanalysts explain to us that our dreams are the very opposite of a free flow of images. When these express some fundamental desire, it is in order perforce to cross the threshold of the super-ego, hiding behind the mark of a two-fold symbolism, one general, the other individual. But this censorship is not something negative. Without it, without the resistance it offers to the imagination, dreams would not exist.

There is only one way to think of *Miracolo a Milano,* namely as a reflection, on the level of a film dream, and through the medium of the social symbolism of contemporary Italy, of the warm heart of Vittorio De Sica. This would explain what seems bizarre and inorganic in this strange film: otherwise it is hard to understand the gaps in its dramatic continuity and its indifference to all narrative logic.

In passing, we might note how much the cinema owes to a love for living creatures. There is no way of completely understanding the art of Flaherty, Renoir, Vigo, and especially Chaplin unless we try to discover beforehand what particular kind of tenderness, of sensual or sentimental affection, they reflect. In my opinion, the cinema more than any other art is particularly bound up with love. The novelist in his relations to his characters needs intelligence more than love; understanding is his form of loving. If the art of a Chaplin were transposed into literature, it would tend to lapse into sentimentality; that is why a man like André Suarès, a man of letters *par excellence,* and evidently impervious to the poetry of the cinema, can talk about the "ignoble heart" of Chaplin when this heart brings to the cinema the nobility of myth. Every art and every stage in the evolution of each art has its specific scale of values. The tender, amused sensuality of Renoir, the more heart-rending tenderness of Vigo, achieve on the screen a tone and an accent which no other medium of expression could give them. Between such feelings and the cinema there exists a mysterious affinity which is sometimes denied even to the greatest of men. No one better than De Sica can lay claim to being the successor to Chaplin. We have already remarked how as an actor he has a quality of presence, a light which subtly transforms both the scenario and the other actors to such an extent that no one can pretend to play opposite De Sica as he would opposite someone else. We in France have not hitherto known the brilliant actor who appeared in Camerini's films. He had to become famous as a director before he was noticed by the public. By then he no longer had the physique of a young leading man, but his charm survived, the more remarkable for being the less easy to explain. Even when appearing as just a simple actor in the films of other directors, De Sica was already himself a director since his presence modified the film and influenced its style. Chaplin concentrates on himself and within himself the radiation of his tenderness, which means that cruelty is not always excluded from his world; on the contrary, it has a necessary and dialectic relationship to love, as is evident from *Monsieur Verdoux.* Charlie is goodness itself, projected onto the world. He is ready to love everything, but the world does not always respond. On the other hand, De Sica the director infuses into his actors the power to love that he himself possesses as an actor. Chaplin also chooses his cast carefully ,but always with an eye to himself and to putting his character in a better light. We find in De Sica the humanity of Chaplin, but shared with the world at large. De Sica possesses the gift of being able to convey an intense sense of the human presence, a disarming grace of expression and of gesture which, in their unique way, are an irresistible testimony to man. Ricci (*Ladri di Biciclette*), Toto (*Miracolo a Milano*), and *Umberto D,* although greatly differing in physique from Chaplin and De Sica, make us think of them.

It would be a mistake to believe that the love De Sica bears for man, and forces us to bear witness to, is a form of optimism. If no one is really bad, if face to face with each individual human being we are forced to drop our accusation, as was Ricci when he caught up with the thief, we are obliged to say that the evil which undeniably does exist in the world is elsewhere than in the heart of man, that it is somewhere in the order of things. One could say it is in society and be partly right. In one way *Ladri di Biciclette, Miracolo a Milano,* and *Umberto D* are indictments of a revolutionary nature. If there were no unemployment it would not be a tragedy to lose one's bicycle. However, this political explanation does not cover the whole drama. De Sica protests the comparison that has been made between *Ladri di Biciclette* and the works of Kafka on the grounds that his hero's alienation is social and not metaphysical. True enough, but Kafka's myths are no less valid if one accepts them as allegories of social alienation, and one does not have to believe in a cruel God to feel the guilt of which Joseph K. is culpable. On the contrary, the drama lies in this: God does not exist, the last office in the castle is empty. Perhaps we have here the particular tragedy of today's world, the raising of a self-deifying social reality to a transcendental state.

The troubles of Bruno and Umberto D have their immediate and evident causes but we also observe that there is an insoluble residue comprised of the psychological and material complexities of our social relationships, which neither the high quality of an institution nor the good will of our neighbors can dispose of. The nature of the latter is positive and social, but its action proceeds always from a necessity that is at once absurd and imperative. This is, in my opinion, what makes this film so great and so rich. It renders a two-fold justice: one by way of an irrefutable description of the wretched condition of the proletariat, another by way of the implicit and constant appeal of a human need that any society whatsoever must respect. It condemns a world in which the poor are obliged to steal from one another to survive (the police protect the rich only too well) but this imposed condemnation is not enough, because it is not only a given historical institution that is in question or a particular economic setup, but the congenital indifference of our social organization, as such, to the fortuitousness of individual happiness. Otherwise Sweden could be the earthly paradise, where bikes are left along the sidewalk both day and night. De Sica loves mankind, his brothers, too much not to want to remove every conceivable cause of their unhappiness, but he also reminds us that every man's happiness is a miracle of love whether in Milan or anywhere else. A society which does not take every opportunity to smother happiness is already better than one which sows hate, but the most perfect still would not create love, for love remains a private matter between man and man. In what country in the world would they keep rabbit hutches in an oil field? In what other would the loss of an administrative document not be as agonizing as the theft of a bicycle? It is part of the realm of politics to think up and promote the objective conditions necessary for human happiness, but it is not part of its essential function to respect its subjective conditions. In the universe of De Sica, there lies a latent pessimism, an unavoidable pessimism we can never be grateful enough to him for, because in it resides the appeal of the potential of man, the witness to his final and irrefutable humanity.

I have used the word love. I should rather have said poetry. These two words are synonymous or at least complementary. Poetry is but the active and creative form of love, its projection into the world. Although spoiled and laid waste by social upheaval, the childhood of the shoeshine boy has retained the power to transform his wretchedness in a dream. In France, in the primary schools, the children are taught to say "Who steals an egg, steals a bull." De Sica's formula is "Who steals an egg is dreaming of a horse." Toto's miraculous gift which was handed on to him by his adopted grandmother is to have retained from childhood an inexhaustible capacity for defense by way of poetry; the piece of business I find most significant in *Miracolo a Milano* is that of Emma Grammatica rushing toward the spilled milk. It does not matter who else scolds Toto for his lack of initiative and wipes up the milk with a cloth, so long as the quick gesture of the old woman has as its purpose to turn the little catastrophe into a marvelous game, a stream in the middle of a landscape of the same proportion. And so on to the multiplication tables, another profound terror of one's childhood, which, thanks to the little old woman, turns into a dream. City dweller Toto names the streets and the squares "four times four is sixteen" or "nine times nine is eighty-one," for these cold mathematical symbols are more beautiful in his eyes than the names of the characters of mythology. Here again we think of Charlie; he also owes to his childhood spirit his remarkable power of transforming the world to a better purpose. When reality resists him and he cannot materially change it—he switches its meaning. Take for example, the dance of the rolls, in *The Gold Rush,* or the shoes in the soup pot, with this proviso that, always on the defensive, Charlie reserves his power of metamorphosis for his own advantage, or, at most, for the benefit of the woman he loves. Toto on the other hand goes out to others. He does not give a moment's thought to any benefit the dove can bring him, his joy lies in his being able to spread joy. When he can no longer do anything for his neighbor he takes it on himself to assume various shapes, now limping for the lame man, making himself small for the dwarf, blind for the one-eyed man. The dove is just an arbitrarily added possibility, to give poetry a material form, because most people need something to assist their imaginations. But Toto does not know what to do with himself unless it is for someone else's benefit.

Zavattini told me once: "I am like a painter standing before a field, who asks himself which blade of grass he should begin with." De Sica is the ideal director for a declaration of faith such as this. There is also the art of the playwright who divides the moments of life into episodes which, in

75

respect of the moments lived, are what the blades of grass are to the field. To paint every blade of grass one must be the Douanier Rousseau. In the world of cinema one must have the love of a De Sica for creation itself.

A Note on Umberto D

Until I saw *Umberto D,* I considered *Ladri di Biciclette* as having reached the uttermost limits of neorealism so far as the concept of narrative is concerned. It seems to me today that *Ladri di Biciclette* falls far short of the ideal Zavattini subject. Not that I consider *Umberto D* superior. The unmatchable superiority of *Ladri di Biciclette* still resides in the paradox of its having reconciled radically opposite values: factual freedom and narrative discipline. But the authors only achieve this by sacrificing the continuum of reality. In *Umberto D* one catches a glimpse, on a number of occasions, of what a truly realist cinema of time could be, a cinema of "duration."

These experiments in continuous time are not new in cinema. Alfred Hitchcock's *Rope,* for example, runs for eighty uninterrupted minutes. But there it was just a question of action such as we have in the theater. The real problem is not the continuity of the exposed film but the temporal structure of the incident.

Rope could be filmed without a change of focus, without any break in the shots, and still provide a dramatic spectacle, because in the original play the incidents were already set in order dramatically according to an artificial time—theatrical time—just as there is musical time and dance time.

In at least two scenes of *Umberto D* the problem of subject and script take on a different aspect. In these instances it is a matter of making "life time"—the simple continuing to be of a person to whom nothing in particular happens—take on the quality of a spectacle, of a drama. I am thinking in particular of when Umberto D goes to bed, having retired to his room thinking he has a fever and, especially, of the little servant girl's awakening in the morning. These two sequences undoubtedly constitute the ultimate in "performance" of a certain kind of cinema, at the level of what one would call "the invisible subject," by which I mean the subject entirely dissolved in the fact to which it has given rise; while when a film is taken from a story, the latter continues to survive by itself like a skeleton without its muscles; one can always "tell" the story of the film.

The function of the subject is here no less essential than the story but its essence is reabsorbed into the scenario. To put it another way, the subject exists before the working scenario, but it does not exist afterward. Only the "fact" exists which the subject had itself forecast. If I try to recount the film to someone who has not seen it—for example what Umberto D is doing in his room or the little servant Maria in the kitchen, what is there left for me to describe? An impalpable show of gestures without meaning, from which the person I am talking to cannot derive the slightest idea of the emotion that gripped the viewer. The subject here is sacrificed beforehand, like the wax in the casting of the bronze.

At the scenario level this type of subject corresponds, reciprocally, to the scenario based entirely on the behavior of the actor. Since the real time of the narrative is not that of the drama but the concrete duration of the character, this objectiveness can only be transformed into a *mise en scène* (scenario and action) in terms of something totally subjective. I mean by this that the film is identical with what the actor is doing and with this alone. The outside world is reduced to being an accessory to this pure action, which is sufficient to itself in the same way that algae deprived of air produce the oxygen they need. The actor who gives a representation of a particular action, who "interprets a part" always, in a measure, directs himself because he is calling more or less on a system of generally accepted dramatic conventions which are learned in conservatories. Not even these conventions are any help to him here. He is entirely in the hands of the director in this complete replica of life.

True, *Umberto D* is not a perfect film like *Ladri di Biciclette,* but this is perhaps understandable since its ambition was greater. Less perfect in its entirety but certainly more perfect and more unalloyed in some of its parts—those in which De Sica and Zavattini exhibit complete fidelity to the aesthetic of neorealism. That is why one must not accuse *Umberto D* of facile sentimentality, some measure of modest appeal to social pity. The good qualities and even, for that matter, the defects of the film are far beyond any categories of morality or politics. We are dealing here with a cinematographic "report," a disconcerting and irrefutable observation on the human condition. One may or may not find it to one's taste that this report should be made on the life of a minor functionary boarding with a family or on a little pregnant servant; but, certainly, what we have just learned about this old man and this girl as revealed through their accidental misfortunes above all concerns the human condition. I have no hesitation in stating that the cinema has rarely gone such a long way toward making us aware of what it is to be a man. (And also, for that matter, of what it is to be a dog.)

Hitherto dramatic literature has provided us with a doubtless exact knowledge of the human soul, but one which stands in the same relation to man as classical physics to matter—what scientists call macrophysics, useful only for phenomena of considerable magnitude. And certainly the novel has gone to extremes in categorizing this knowledge. The emotional physics of a Proust is microscopic. But the matter with which this microphysics is concerned is on the inside. It is memory. The cinema is not necessarily a substitute for the novel in this search after man, but it has at least one advantage over it, namely, that it presents man only in the present—to the "time lost and found" of Proust there corresponds in a measure the "time discovered" of Zavattini; this is, in the contemporary cinema, something like Proust in the present indicative tense.

UMBERTO D: A GREAT WORK

MIRACOLO IN MILANO created only discord. In the absence of the general enthusiasm that greeted *Ladri di Biciclette* the originality of the scenario, the mixture of the fantastic and the commonplace, and the penchant of our time for political cryptography stirred up around this strange film a sort of *succès de scandale* (which Micheline Vian has debunked with relentless humor in an excellent article published in *Les Temps modernes).*

A conspiracy of silence, a sullen and obstinate reticence, is building up against *Umberto D* and as a result even the good that has been written about it seems to condemn the film with faint praise; though it is a kind of mute ill humor or even contempt (to which no one is prepared to admit in view of the illustrious past of its makers) that in secret animates the hostility of more than one critic. There will certainly be no "Battle of *Umberto D."*

And yet it is one of the most revolutionary and courageous films of the last two years—not only of the Italian cinema but of European cinema as a whole, a masterpiece to which film history is certainly going to grant a place of honor, even if for the moment an inexplicable failure of attention or a certain blindness on the part of those who love the cinema allows it only a reluctant and ineffective esteem.

If there are lines outside theaters showing *Adorables créatures* or *Le Fruit défendu,* it is perhaps in part because the brothels have been closed;

all the same, there should be a few tens of thousands of people in Paris who expect other pleasures from film.

For the Paris public to be properly shamed, must *Umberto D* leave the marquees before it has had the kind of run it deserves?

The chief reason for the misunderstandings that have arisen about *Umberto D* lies in comparing it with *Ladri di Biciclette*. Some will say with some semblance of reason that De Sica "returns to neorealism" here, after the poetico-realist interlude of *Miracolo in Milano*. This is true, but only if one hastens to add that the perfection of *Ladri di Biciclette* was only a beginning, though it was first regarded as a culmination. It took *Umberto D* to make us understand what it was in the realism of *Ladri di Biciclette* that was still a concession to classical dramaturgy. Consequently what is so unsettling about *Umberto D* is primarily the way it rejects any relationship to traditional film spectacle.

Of course, if we take just the theme of the film we can reduce it to a seemingly "populist" melodrama with social pretensions, an appeal on behalf of the middle class: a retired minor official reduced to penury decides against suicide because he can neither find someone to take care of his dog nor pluck up enough courage to kill it before he kills himself. This final episode is not the moving conclusion to a dramatic series of events. If the classical concept of "construction" still has some meaning here, the sequence of events which De Sica reports obeys a necessity that has nothing to do with dramatic structure. What kind of causal relationship could you establish between a harmless angina for which *Umberto D* will be treated in hospital, his landlady's turning him out on the street, and his thinking of suicide? The notice to vacate was served irrespective of the angina. A "dramatic author" would have made the angina acute in order to establish a logical and a pathetic relationship between the two things. Here, on the contrary, the period in hospital is in effect hardly justified by the real state of Umberto D's health; rather than making us pity him for his unhappy lot, it is really a rather cheerful episode. That is not where the question lies, though. It is not his real poverty that moves Umberto D to despair, though it is in a very real sense a contributing factor, but only in the degree that it shows him just how lonely he is. The few things which Umberto D must rely on others to do for him are all it takes to alienate his few human contacts. To the extent that it is indeed the middle class that is involved, the film reports the secret misery, the egoism, the lack of fellow-feeling which characterizes its members. Its protagonist advances step by step further into his solitude: the person closest to him, the only one to show him any tenderness, is his landlady's little maid; but her kindness and her goodwill cannot prevail over her worries as an unwed mother-to-be. Through his one friendship, then, there runs the motif of despair.

But here I am now lapsing back into traditional critical concepts, though I am talking about a film whose originality I set out to prove.

If one assumes some distance from the story and can still see in it a dramatic patterning, some general development in character, a single general trend in its component events, this is only after the fact. The narrative unit is not the episode, the event, the sudden turn of events, or the character of its protagonists; it is the succession of concrete instants of life, no one of which can be said to be more important than another, for their ontological equality destroys drama at its very basis. One wonderful sequence— it will remain one of the high points of film—is a perfect illustration of this approach to narrative and thus to direction: the scene in which the maid gets up. The camera confines itself to watching her doing her little chores: moving around the kitchen still half asleep, drowning the ants that have invaded the sink, grinding the coffee. The cinema here is conceived as the exact opposite of that "art of ellipsis" to which we are much too ready to believe it devoted. Ellipsis is a narrative process; it is logical in nature and so it is abstract as well; it presupposes analysis and choice; it organizes the facts in accord with the general dramatic direction to which it forces them to submit. On the contrary, De Sica and Zavattini attempt to divide the event up into still smaller events and these into events smaller still, to the extreme limits of our capacity to perceive them in time. Thus, the unit event in a classical film would be "the maid's getting out of bed"; two or three brief shots would suffice to show this. De Sica replaces this narrative unit with a series of "smaller" events: she wakes up; she crosses the hall; she drowns the ants; and so on. But let us examine just one of these. We see how the grinding of the coffee is divided in turn into a series of independent moments; for example, when she shuts the door with the tip of her outstretched foot. As it goes in on her the camera follows the movement of her leg so that the image finally concentrates on her toes feeling the surface of the door. Have I already said that it is Zavattini's dream to make a whole film out of ninety minutes in the life of a man to whom nothing happens? That is precisely what "neorealism" means for for him. Two or three sequences in *Umberto D* give us more than a glimpse of what such a film might be like; they are fragments of it that have already been shot. But let us make no mistake about the meaning and the value realism has here. De Sica and Zavattini are concerned to make cinema the asymptote of reality—but in order that it should ultimately be life itself that becomes spectacle, in order that life might in this perfect mirror be visible poetry, be the self into which film finally changes it.*

---

* "Telle qu'en elle-même, enfin, le cinéma la change." Bazin here rewrites the first line of Mallarmé's famous sonnet *Tombeau d'Edgar Poe*, "Tel qu'en lui-même, enfin, l'éternité le change."

CABIRIA: THE
VOYAGE TO THE END OF NEOREALISM

As I sit down to write this article, I have no idea what kind of reception Fellini's latest film will have. I hope it is as enthusiastic as I think it should be, but I do not conceal from myself the fact that there are two categories of viewers who may have reservations about the film. The first is that segment of the general public likely to be put off by the way the story mixes the strange with what seems to be an almost melodramatic naïvete. These people can accept the theme of the whore with a heart of gold only if it is spiced with crime. The second belongs, albeit reluctantly, to that part of the "elite" which supports Fellini almost in spite of itself. Constrained to admire *La Strada* and under even more constraint from its austerity and its "outcast" status to admire *Il Bidone,* I expect these viewers now to criticize *Le Notti di Cabiria* for being "too well made"—a film in which practically nothing is left to chance, a film that is clever—artful. even. Let's forget the first objection; it is important only in the effect it may have at the box office. The second, however, is worth refuting.

The least surprising thing about *Le Notti di Cabiria* is not that this is the first time Fellini has succeeded in putting together a masterly script, with an action that cannot be faulted—unmarred by clichés or missing links, one in which there could be no place for the unhappy cuts and the corrections in editing from which *La Strada* and *Il Bidone* suffered.* Of course, *Lo Sceicco bianco* and even *I Vitelloni* were not clumsy in their construction, but chiefly because, though their themes were specifically Fellinian, they were still being expressed within a framework provided by relatively traditional scenarios. Fellini has finally cast these crutches aside with *La Strada*: theme and character alone are the final determinants in the story now, to the exclusion of all else; story has nothing now to do with what one calls plot; I even have doubts that it is proper here to speak of "action." The same is true of *Il Bidone*.

It is not that Fellini would like to return to the excuses which drama affords him in his earlier films. Quite the contrary. *Le Notti di Cabiria* goes even beyond *Il Bidone,* but here the contradictions between what I will call the "verticality" of its author's themes and the "horizontality" of the requirements of narrative have been reconciled. It is within the Fellinian system that he now finds his solutions. This does not prevent the viewer from possibly mistaking brilliant perfection for mere facility, if not indeed for betrayal. All the same, on one score at least Fellini has deceived himself a little: is he not counting on the character played by François Perier (who to me seems miscast) to have a surprise effect? Now it is clear that any effect of "suspense" or even of "drama" is essentially alien to the Fellinian system, in which it is impossible for time ever to serve as an abstract or dynamic support—as an *a priori* framework for narrative structure. In *La Strada* as in *Il Bidone,* time is nothing more than the shapeless framework modified by fortuitous events which affect the fate of his heroes, though never in consequence of external necessity. Events do not "happen" in Fellini's world; they "befall" its inhabitants; that is to say, they occur as an effect of "vertical" gravity, not in conformity to the laws

---

* Alas, the facts give me the lie: the original-language version shown in Paris reveals the deletion of at least one long scene that was still in the film when it was shown at Cannes, namely the scene of "the visitor of Saint Vincent de Paul" to which I allude below. But then we have seen how easy it has been in the past to convince Fellini—if it is indeed he who is responsible for this cut—that a truly remarkable sequence is "useless." [The "visitor" is a member of the Society of Saint Vincent de Paul founded in France in 1833 to care for the sick, the aged, the poor, and what were then known as "fallen women."—TR.]

of "horizontal" causality. As for the characters themselves, they exist and change only in reference to a purely internal kind of time—which I cannot qualify even as Bergsonian, in so far as Bergson's theory of the *Données immédiates de la conscience* contains a strong element of psychologism. Let us avoid the vague terms of a "spiritualizing" vocabulary. Let us not say that the transformation of the characters takes place at the level of the "soul." But it has at least to occur at that depth of their being into which consciousness only occasionally reaches down. This does not mean at the level of the unconscious or the subconscious but rather the level on which what Jean-Paul Sartre calls the "basic project" obtains, the level of ontology. Thus the Fellinian character does not evolve; he ripens or at the most becomes transformed (whence the metaphor of the angel's wings, to which I will shortly return).

A Spurious Melodrama

But let us confine ourselves, for the moment, to the structure of the script. I totally reject, then, the *coup de théâtre* in *Le Notti di Cabiria* which belatedly reveals Oscar a swindler. Fellini must have been aware of what he was doing because, as if to compound his sin, he makes François Perier wear dark glasses when he is about to turn "wicked." What of it? This is a minor concession indeed and I find it easy to pardon in view of the care Fellini now takes to avoid in this film the grave danger to which a complicated and much too facile shooting script exposed him in *Il Bidone*.

I find it all the more easy to pardon when it is the only concession he makes in this film; for the rest Fellini communicates the tension and the rigor of tragedy to it without ever having to fall back on devices alien to his universe. Cabiria, the little prostitute whose simple soul is rooted in hope, is not a character out of melodrama, because her desire to "get out" is not motivated by the ideals of bourgeois morality or a strictly bourgeois sociology. She does not hold her trade in contempt. As a matter of fact, if there were such creatures as pure-hearted pimps capable of understanding her and of embodying not love indeed but just a belief in life, she would doubtless see no incompatibility between her secret hopes and her nighttime activities. Does she not owe one of her greatest moments of happiness—happiness followed consequently by an even more bitter deception—to her chance meeting with a famous film star who because he is drunk and feeling embittered against love proposes to take her home to his luxurious apartment. There was something to make the other girls just die of envy! But the incident is fated to come to a pitiful end, because after all a prostitute's trade commonly destines her only to disappointments; this is why she longs, more or less consciously, to get out of it through the impossible love of some stalwart fellow who will make no demands of her. If we seem now to have reached an outcome typical of bourgeois melodrama, it is in any case by a very different route.

Le Notti di Cabiria—like *La Strada,* like *Il Bidone,* and, in the final analysis, like *I Vitelloni*—is the story of *ascesis,* of renunciation, and, (however you choose to interpret the term) of salvation. The beauty and the rigor of its construction proceed this time from the perfect economy of its constituent episodes. Each of them, as I have said earlier, exists by and for itself, unique and colorful as an event, but now each belongs to an order of things that never fails to reveal itself in retrospect as having been absolutely necessary. As she goes from hope to hope, plumbing enroute the depths of betrayal, contempt, and poverty, Cabiria follows a path on which every halt readies her for the stage ahead. When one stops and reflects, one realizes that there is nothing in the film, before the meeting with the benefactor of the tramps (whose irruption into the film seems at first sight to be no more than a characteristic piece of Fellinian bravura), which is not proved subsequently to be necessary to trick Cabiria into making an act of ill-placed faith; for if such men do exist, then every miracle is possible and we, too, will be without mistrust when Perier appears.

I do not intend to repeat what has been written about Fellini's message. It has, anyway, been noticeably the same since *I Vitelloni.* This is not to be taken as a sign of sterility. On the contrary, while variety is the mark of a "director," it is unity of inspiration that connotes the true "author." But in the light of this new masterpiece maybe I can still attempt to throw a little more light on what in essence is Fellini's style.

A Realism of Appearances

It is absurd, preposterous even, to deny him a place among the neorealists. Such a judgment could only be possible on ideological grounds. It is true that Fellini's realism though social in origin is not social in intent. This remains as individual as it is in Chekhov or Dostoievsky. Realism, let me repeat, is to be defined not in terms of ends but of means, and neorealism by a specific kind of relationship of means to ends. What De Sica has in common with Rossellini and Fellini is obviously not the deep meaning of their films—even if, as it happens, these more or less coincide —but the pride of place they all give to the representation of reality at the expense of dramatic structures. To put it more precisely, the Italian cinema has replaced a "realism" deriving in point of content from the naturalism of novels and structurally from theater with what, for brevity's sake, we shall call "phenomenological" realism which never "adjusts" reality to meet the needs imposed by psychology or drama. The relation between meaning and appearance having been in a sense inverted, appearance is always presented as a unique discovery, an almost documentary revelation that retains its full force of vividness and detail. Whence the director's art lies in the skill with which he compels the event to reveal its meaning— or at least the meaning he lends it—without removing any of its ambiguity.* Thus defined, neorealism is not the exclusive property of any one ideology nor even of any one ideal, no more than it excludes any other ideal—no more, in point of fact, than reality excludes anything.

I even tend to view Fellini as the director who goes the farthest of any to date in this neorealist asethetic, who goes even so far that he goes all the way through it and finds himself on the other side.

Let us consider how free Fellini's direction is from the encumbrances

---

* For Bazin's use of the term "ambiguity," see the Introduction.

of psychological after-effects. His characters are never defined by their "character" but exclusively by their appearance. I deliberately avoid the world "behavior" because its meaning has become too restricted; the way people behave is only one element in the knowledge we have of them. We know them by many other signs, not only their faces, of course, but by the way they move, by everything that makes the body the outer shell of the inner man—even more, perhaps, by things still more external than these, things on the frontier between the individual and the world, things such as haircut, moustache, clothing, eye glasses (the one prop that Fellini has used to a point where it has become a gimmick). Then, beyond that again, setting, too, has a role to play—not, of course, in an expressionistic sense but rather as establishing a harmony or a disharmony between setting and character. I am thinking in particular of the extraordinary relationship established between Cabiria and the unaccustomed settings into which Nazzari inveigles her, the nightclub and the luxurious apartment.

On the Other Side of Things

But it is here that we reach the boundaries of realism, here, too, that Fellini, who drives on further still, takes us beyond them. It is a little as if, having been led to this degree of interest in appearances, we were now to see the characters no longer *among* the objects but, as if these had become transparent, *through* them. I mean by this that without our noticing the world has moved from meaning to analogy, then from analogy to identification with the supernatural. I apologize for this equivocal word; the reader may replace it with whatever he will—"poetry" or "surrealism" or "magic"—whatever the term that expresses the hidden accord which things maintain with an invisible counterpart of which they are, so to speak, merely the adumbration.

Let us take one example from among many others of this process of "supernaturalization," which is to be found in the metaphor of the angel. From his first films, Fellini has been haunted by the angelizing of his characters, as if the angelic state were the ultimate referent in his universe, the final measure of being. One can trace this tendency in its explicit development at least from *I Vitelloni* on: Sordi dresses up for the carnival as a guardian angel; a little later on what Fabrizi steals, as if by chance, is the carved wooden statue of an angel. But these allusions are direct and concrete. Subtler still, and all the more interesting because it seems unconscious, is the shot in which the monk who has come down from working in a tree loads a long string of little branches on his back. This detail is nothing more than a nice "realistic" touch for us, perhaps even for Fellini himself, until at the end of *Il Bidone* we see Antonio dying at the side of the road: in the white light of dawn he sees a procession of children and women bearing bundles of sticks on their backs: angels pass! I must note, too, how in the same film Picasso races down a street and the tails of his raincoat spread out behind him like little wings. It is that same Richard Basehart again who appears before Gelsomina as if he were weightless, a dazzling sight on his high wire under the spotlights.

There is no end to Fellini's symbolism. Certainly, it would be possible to study the whole body of his work from this one angle.* What needed to be done was simply to place it within the context of the logic of neorealism, for it is evident that these associations of objects and characters which constitute Fellini's universe derive their value and their importance from realism alone—or, to put it a better way, perhaps, from the objectivity with which they are recorded. It is not in order to look like an angel that the friar carries his bundles of sticks on his back, but it is enough to see the wing in the twigs for the old monk to be transformed into one. One might say that Fellini is not opposed to realism, any more than he is to neorealism, but rather that he achieves it surpassingly in a poetic reordering of the world.

A Revolution in Narrative

Fellini creates a similar revolution at the narrative level. From this point of view, to be sure, neorealism is also a revolution in form which comes to bear on content. For example, the priority which they accord incident

---

* See the article by Dominique Aubier in *Cahiers du Cinéma,* No. 49.

over plot has led De Sica and Zavattini to replace plot as such with a microaction based on an infinitely divisible attention to the complexities in even the most ordinary of events. This in itself rules out the slightest hierarchy, whether psychological, dramatic, or ideological, among the incidents that are portrayed. This does not mean, of course, that the director is obliged to renounce all choice over what he is to show us, but it does mean that he no longer makes the choice in reference to some pre-existing dramatic organization. In this new perspective, the important sequence can just as well be the long scene that "serves no purpose" by traditional screenplay standards.*

Nonetheless—this is true even of *Umberto D*, which perhaps represents the limits of experimentation in this new dramaturgy—the evolution of film follows an invisible thread. Fellini, I think, brings the neorealist revolution to its point of perfection when he introduces a new kind of script, the scenario lacking any dramatic linking, based as it is, to the exclusion of all else, on the phenomenological description of the characters. In the films of Fellini, the scenes that establish the logical relations, the significant changes of fortune, the major points of dramatic articulation, only provide the continuity links, while the long descriptive sequences, seeming to exercise no effect on the unfolding of the "action" proper, constitute the truly important and revealing scenes. In *I Vitelloni*, these are the nocturnal walks, the senseless strolls on the beach; in *La Strada*, the visit to the convent; in *Il Bidone*, the evening at the nightclub or the New Year's celebration. It is not when they are doing something specific that Fellini's characters best reveal themselves to the viewer but by their endless milling around.

If there are, still, tensions and climaxes in the films of Fellini which leave nothing to be desired as regards drama or tragedy, it is because, in the absence of traditional dramatic causality, the incidents in his films develop effects of analogy and echo. Fellini's hero never reaches the final crisis (which destroys him and saves him) by a progressive dramatic linking but because the circumstances somehow or other affect him, build up in-

---

* This is true of the sequence that has been deleted from the film.

side him like the vibrant energy in a resonating body. He does not develop; he is transformed; overturning finally like an iceberg whose center of buoyancy has shifted unseen.

Eye to Eye

By way of conclusion, and to compress the disturbing perfection of *Le Notti di Cabiria* into a single phrase, I would like to analyze the final shot of the film, which strikes me, when everything else is taken into account, as the boldest and the most powerful shot in the whole of Fellini's work. Cabiria, stripped of everything—her money, her love, her faith—emptied now of herself, stands on a road without hope. A group of boys and girls swarm into the scene singing and dancing as they go, and from the depths of her nothingness Cabiria slowly returns to life; she starts to smile again; soon she is dancing, too. It is easy to imagine how artificial and symbolic this ending would have been, casting aside as it does all the objections of verisimilitude, if Fellini had not succeeded in projecting his film onto a higher plane by a single detail of direction, a stroke of real genius that forces us suddenly to identify with his heroine. Chaplin's name is often mentioned in conection with *La Strada*, but I have never thought the comparison between Gelsomina and Charlie (which I find hard to take in itself) very convincing. The first shot which is not only up to Chaplin's level but the true equal of his best inventions is the final shot of *Le Notti di Cabiria,* when Giulietta Masina turns toward the camera and her glance crosses ours. As far as I know, Chaplin is the only man in the history of film who made successful systematic use of this gesture, which the books about filmmaking are unanimous in condemning. Nor would it be in place if when she looked us in the eye Cabiria seemed to come bearing some ultimate truth. But the finishing touch to this stroke of directorial genius is this, that Cabiria's glance falls several times on the camera without ever quite coming to rest there. The lights go up on this marvel of ambiguity. Cabiria is doubtless still the heroine of the adventures which she has been living out before us, somewhere behind that screen, but here she is now inviting us, too, with her glance to follow her on the road to which she is about to return. The invitation is chaste, discreet, and indefinite enough that we can pretend to think that she means to be looking at somebody else. At the same time, though, it is definite and direct enough, too, to remove us quite finally from our role of spectator.

IN DEFENSE OF ROSSELLINI

A letter to Guido Aristarco, editor-in-chief
of CINEMA NUOVO

My dear Aristarco,

I have been meaning to write these comments for some time now, but month after month I have deferred doing so, put off by the importance of the problem and its many ramifications. I am also aware that I lack theoretical preparation, as compared with the seriousness and thoroughness with which Italian critics on the left devote themselves to the study of neorealism in depth. Although I welcomed neorealism on its first arrival in France and have ever since continued to devote to it the unstinting best of my critical attentions, I cannot claim to have a coherent theory to rival your own, nor can I pretend to be able to situate the phenomenon of neorealism in the history of Italian culture as surely as you can. If you take into account, too, the fact that I am bound to look absurd if I try to instruct Italians in their own cinema, you will have the major reasons why I have failed as yet to respond to your invitation to discuss in the pages of *Cinema Nuovo* the critical position which you and your associates have taken on some recent films.

I would like to remind you, before getting to the heart of the discussion, that differences of opinion due to nationality are frequent even among critics of the same generation whom all else would seem to align. We of *Cahiers du Cinéma*, for example, have experienced this with the staff of *Sight and Sound*, and I am not ashamed to admit that it was at least in part the high regard in which Lindsay Anderson held Jacques Becker's *Casque d'or* (which was a failure in France) that led me to reconsider my own view and to see virtues in the film which had escaped me. It is true that the judgment of a foreigner is apt sometimes to go astray because of a lack of familiarity with the context from which a film comes. For example, the success outside France of films by Duvivier or Pagnol is clearly the result of a misunderstanding. Foreign critics admire in these films a picture of France which seems to them "wonderfully typical," and they confuse this "exoticism" with the value of these films as film. I recognize that these differences are of little consquence and I presume that the success abroad of some Italian films which I think you are right to hold in low esteem is based on the same kind of misunderstanding. Nevertheless, I do not think that this is true of the films that have caused us to disagree, nor even with neorealism in general.

To begin with, you will allow that French critics were not wrong, at the very outset, in being more enthusiastic than Italian critics about the films that today are the undisputed glory of the Italian cinema on both sides of the Alps. For my part, I flatter myself that I was one of the few French critics who always linked the rebirth of Italian cinema to "neorealism," even at the time when it was fashionable to say that the term was meaningless. Today I still think it the best term there is to designate what is best and most creative in Italian cinema.

But this is also why I am disturbed by the way in which you defend it. Do I dare suggest, dear Aristarco, that the harsh line taken by *Cinema Nuovo* against certain tendencies in neorealism which you consider regressive prompts me to fear that you are thereby unwittingly putting the knife to what is most alive and rich in your cinema? I am eclectic enough in what I most admire in Italian cinema, but you have passed some harsh judgments which I am prepared to accept: you are an Italian. I can understand why the success in France of *Pane, Amore e Fantasie* annoys you; your reaction resembles mine to Duvivier's films on Paris. But, on the other hand, when I find you hunting for fleas in Gelsomina's tousled hair, or dismissing Rossellini's last film as less than nothing I am forced to conclude that under the guise of theoretical integrity you are in the process of nipping in the bud some of the liveliest and most promising offshoots of what I persist in calling neorealism.

You tell me you are amazed at the relative success which *Viaggio in Italia* has had in Paris, and even more so by the almost unanimous enthusiasm of the French critics for it. As for *La Strada*, you are well aware what a success it has been. These two films have come just at the right moment to restore Italian cinema not only in the interest of the general public but also in the esteem of the intellectuals—for interest in Italian film has flagged in the past year or two. The reasons for their success are in many ways very different. Nevertheless, far from their having been felt here as a break with neorealism and still less as a regression, they have given us a feeling of a creative inventiveness deriving directly from the spirit which informs the Italian school. I will try to tell you why.

But I have first to confess to a strong dislike for a notion of neorealism which is based, to the exclusion of all else, on what is only one of its present aspects, for this is to submit its future potential to *a priori* restrictions. Perhaps I dislike it so because I haven't enough of a head for theory. I think, however, that it is because I prefer to allow art its natural freedom. In sterile periods theory is a fruitful source for the analysis of the causes of the drought, and it can help to create the conditions necessary for the rebirth. But when we have had the good fortune to witness the wonderful flowering of Italian cinema over the past ten years, is there not more danger than advantage to be gained if we try to lay down a law which we say is imposed by theory? Not that we do not have to be strict. On the contrary, an exacting and rigorous criticism is needed—now more than ever, I think. But its concern should be to denounce commercial compromise, demagoguery, the lowering of the level of the ambitions, rather than to impose *a priori* aesthetic standards on artists. As I view it, a director whose aesthetic ideals are close to your own but who sets to work assuming that he can include only 10 or 20 per cent of these ideals in any commercial script he may happen to shoot has less merit than a man who for better or worse makes films that conform to his ideal, even if his concept of neorealism differs from yours. In the first of these two films, now, you are content objectively to record that the film is at least in part free of compromise by according it two stars in your critiques, but you consign the second film to your aesthetic hell, without right of appeal.

In your view Rossellini would, doubtless, be less to blame if he had made something like *Stazione Termini* or *Umberto D* rather than *Giovanna d'Arco al rogo* or *La Paura*. It is not my intention to defend the author of *Europa 51* at the expense of Lattuada or De Sica; the policy of compromise is defensible, up to a point; I am not going to try to define it here, but it does seem to me that Rossellini's independence gives his work —whatever one may think of it on other grounds—an integrity of style and a moral unity only too rare in cinema, which compel us to esteem it even before we admire it.

But it is not on such methodological grounds as these that I hope to defend him. Instead, I will direct my argument on his behalf at the assumptions on which the discussion is based. Has Rossellini ever really been a neorealist and is he one still? It would seem to me that you admit that he has been a neorealist. How indeed can there be any question of the role played by *Roma Città Aperta* and *Paisà* in the origin and development of neorealism? But you say that a certain "regression" is already apparent in *Allemania Anno Zero,* that it is decisive beginning with *Stromboli* and *I Fioretti di San Francisco,* and that it has become catastrophic in *Europa 51* and *Viaggio in Italia.*

But what is it, in essence that you find to blame in this aesthetic itinerary? Increasingly less concern for social realism, for chronicling the events of daily life, in favor, it is not to be denied, of an increasingly obvious moral message—a moral message that, depending on the degree of his malevolence, a person may identify with either one of the two major tendencies in Italian politics. I refuse to allow the discussion to descend to this dubious level. Even if Rossellini had in fact Christian-Democrat leanings (and of this there is no proof, public or private, so far as I know) this would not be enough to exclude him *a priori* from the possibility of being a neorealist artist. But let that pass.

It is true, nonetheless, that one does have a right to reject the moral or spiritual postulate that is increasingly evident in his work, but even so to reject this would not imply rejection of the aesthetic framework within which this message is manifest unless the films of Rossellini were in fact films *à thèse*, that is, unless they were mere dramatizations of *a priori* ideas. But in point of fact there is no Italian director in whose work aims and form are more closely linked and it is precisely on this basis that I would characterize Rossellini's neorealism.

If the word has any meaning—whatever the differences that arise over its interpretation, above and beyond a minimal agreement—in the first place it stands in opposition to the traditional dramatic systems and also to the various other known kinds of realism in literature and film with which we are familiar, through its claim that there is a certain "wholeness" to reality. I borrow this definition, which I consider to be as correct as it is convenient, from Amedée Ayfre (*Cahiers du Cinéma,* No. 17). Neorealism is a description of reality conceived as a whole by a consciousness disposed to see things as a whole. Neorealism contrasts with the realist aesthetics that preceded it, and in particular with naturalism and verism, in that its realism is not so much concerned with the choice of subject as with a particular way of regarding things. If you like, what is realist in *Paisà* is the Italian Resistance, but what is neorealist is Rossellini's direction—his presentation of the events, a presentation which is at once elliptic and synthetic.

To put it still another way, neorealism by definition rejects analysis, whether political, moral, psychological, logical, or social, of the characters and their actions. It looks on reality as a whole, not incomprehensible, certainly, but inseparably one. This is why neorealism, although not necessarily antispectacular (though spectacle is to all intents and purposes alien to it) is at least basically antitheatrical in the degree that stage acting presupposes on the part of the actor a psychological analysis of the emotions to which a character is subject and a set of expressive physical signs that symbolize a whole range of moral categories.

This does not at all mean that neorealism is limited to some otherwise indefinable "documentarism."* Rossellini is fond of saying that a love not

---

* "Documentarism" according to A. Ayfre is an "attitude supposedly of passivity that claims to be impersonally objective."—TR.

only for his characters but for the real world just as it is lies at the heart of his conception of the way a film is to be directed, and that it is precisely this love that precludes him from putting asunder what reality has joined together, namely, the character and the setting. Neorealism, then, is not characterized by a refusal to take a stand *vis-à-vis* the world, still less by a refusal to judge it; as a matter of fact, it always presupposes an attitude of mind: it is always reality as it is visible through an artist, as refracted by his consciousness—but by his consciousness as a whole and not by his reason alone or his emotions or his beliefs—and reassembled from its distinguishable elements. I would put it this way: the traditional realist artist —Zola, for example—analyzes reality into parts which he then reassembles in a synthesis the final determinant of which is his moral conception of the world, whereas the consciousness of the neorealist director *filters* reality. Undoubtedly, his consciousness, like that of everyone else, does not admit reality as a whole, but the selection that does occur is neither logical nor is it psychological; it is ontological, in the sense that the image of reality it restores to us is still a whole—just as a black-and-white photograph is not an image of reality broken down and put back together again "without the color" but rather a true imprint of reality, a kind of luminous mold in which color simply does not figure. There is ontological identity between the object and its photographic image.

I may perhaps make myself better understood by an example—from *Viaggio in Italia*. Admittedly the public is easily disappointed by the film in that the Naples which it depicts is incomplete. This reality is only a small part of the reality that might have been shown, but the little one sees— statues in a museum, pregnant women, an excavation at Pompeii, the tail-end of the procession of Saint Januarius—has the quality of wholeness which in my view is essential. It is Naples "filtered" through the consciousness of the heroine. If the landscape is bare and confined, it is because the consciousness of an ordinary bourgeoise itself suffers from great spiritual poverty. Nevertheless, the Naples of the film is not false (which it could easily be with the Naples of a documentary three hours long). It is rather a mental landscape at once as objective as a straight photograph and as subjective as pure personal consciousness. We realize now that the attitude which Rossellini takes toward his characters and their geographical and social setting is, at one remove, the attitude of his heroine toward Naples—the difference being that his awareness is that of a highly cultured artist and, in my opinion, an artist of rare spiritual vitality.

I apologize for proceeding by way of metaphor, but I am not a philosopher and I cannot convey my meaning any more directly. I will therefore attempt one more comparison. I will say this of the classical forms of art and of traditional realism, that they are built as houses are built, with bricks or cut stones. It is not a matter of calling into question either the utility of these houses or the beauty they may or may not have, or the perfect suitability of bricks to the building of houses. The reality of the brick lies less in its composition than it does in its form and its strength. It would never enter your head to define it as a piece of clay; its peculiar mineral composition matters little. What does count is that it have the right dimensions. A brick is the basic unit of a house. That this is so is proclaimed by its appearance. One can apply the same argument to the stones of which a bridge is constructed. They fit together perfectly to form an arch. But the big rocks that lie scattered in a ford are now and ever will be no more than mere rocks. Their reality as rocks is not affected when, leaping from one to another, I use them to cross the river. If the service which they have rendered is the same as that of the bridge, it is because I have brought my share of ingenuity to bear on their chance arrangement; I have added the motion which, though it alters neither their nature nor their appearance, gives them a provisional meaning and utility. In the same way, the neorealist film has a meaning, but it is *a posteriori*, to the extent that it permits our awareness to move from one fact to another, from one fragment of reality to the next, whereas in the classical artistic composition the meaning is established *a priori*: the house is already there in the brick.

If my analysis is correct, it follows that the term neorealism should never be used as a noun, except to designate the neorealist directors as a body. Neorealism as such does not exist. There are only neorealist directors—whether they be materialists, Christians, Communists, or whatever. Visconti is neorealistic in *La Terra Trema*, a call to social revolt, and Rossellini is neorealistic in *I Fioretti*, a film which lights up for us a purely spiritual reality. I will only deny the qualification neorealist to the director who, to persuade me, puts asunder what reality has joined together.

In my view, then, *Viaggio in Italia* is neorealist—more so than *L'Oro di Napoli*, for example, which I greatly admire but whose realism is basically psychological and subtly theatrical, despite the many realistic touches that aim to take us in.

I would go even further and claim that of all Italian directors Rossellini has done the most to extend the frontiers of the neorealist aesthetic. I have said that there is no such thing as pure neorealism. The neorealist attitude is an ideal that one can approach to a greater or lesser degree. In all films termed neorealist there are traces still of traditional realism—spectacular, dramatic, or psychological. They can all be broken down into the following components: documentary reality *plus* something else, this something else being the plastic beauty of the images, the social sense, or the poetry, the comedy and so on. You would look in vain in the works of Rossellini for some such distinction of event and intended effect. There is nothing in his films that belongs to literature or to poetry, not even a trace of "the beautiful" in the merely pleasing sense of the word. Rossellini directs facts. It is as if his characters were haunted by some demon of movement. His little brothers of Saint Francis seem to have no better way of glorifying God than to run races. And what of the haunting death march of the little urchin in *Allemania Anno Zero*? Gesture, change, physical movement constitute for Rossellini the essence of human reality. This means, too, that his characters are more apt to be affected by the settings through which they move than the settings are liable to be affected by their movement.

The world of Rossellini is a world of pure acts, unimportant in themselves but preparing the way (as if unbeknownst to God himself) for the sudden dazzling revelation of their meaning. Thus it is with the miracle of *Viaggio in Italia*: unseen by the two leading characters, almost unseen even by the camera, and in any case ambiguous (for Rossellini does not claim that it *is* a miracle but only the noise and crowd movements that people are in the habit of calling a miracle), its impact on the consciousness of the characters is such, nonetheless, as to prompt the unexpected outpouring of their love for one another.

To my mind, no one has been more successful in creating the aesthetic structure which in consequence of its strength, wholeness, and transparency is better suited to the direction of events than the author of *Europa 51*; the structure which Rossellini has created allows the viewer to see nothing but the event itself. This brings to mind the way in which some bodies can exist in either an amorphous or a crystalline state. The art of Rossellini consists in knowing what has to be done to confer on the facts what is at once their most substantial and their most elegant shape—not the most graceful, but the sharpest in outline, the most direct, or the most trenchant. Neorealism discovers in Rossellini the style and the resources of abstraction. To have a regard for reality does not mean that what one does in fact is to pile up appearances. On the contrary, it means that one strips the appearances of all that is not essential, in order to get at the totality in its simplicity. The art of Rossellini is linear and melodic. True, several of his films make one think of a sketch: more is implicit in the line than it actually depicts. But is one to attribute such sureness of line to poverty of invention or to laziness? One would have to say the same of Matisse. Perhaps Rossellini is more a master of line than a painter, more a short-story writer than a novelist. But there is no hierarchy of genres, only of artists.

I do not expect to have convinced you, my dear Aristarco. In any event, it is never with arguments that one wins over a person. The conviction one puts into them often counts for more. I shall be satisfied if just my conviction (in which you will find an echo of the admiration [for Rossellini] of several of my critic colleagues) serves at least to stimulate your own.

THE MYTH OF MONSIEUR VERDOUX

THE ONLY evidence for the indictment and sentencing of Landru (whom a soft-hearted and equivocal popular mythology had promoted to the title of Sire de Gambais) and the sole exhibit that led to his conviction was a small pocket account book. In it he jotted down his expenses with meticulous, detailed conscientiousness. There was recorded, opposite the entry of each final, conjugal trip to the little Norman town where he owned a quiet country house, the cost of two railroad tickets—one a round-trip ticket and the other a one-way. Clearly, from this to an inference of premeditation was but a single step. The *faux-pas* cost Landru his head, and thus we see that there is a boundary beyond which method and system can place their creator in jeopardy. It was Landru's *sang-froid* that was his undoing. Had he attached no greater importance to the crime than to his laundry or his grocery bill, he would perhaps have simply entered the modest expenses of his murders in some general housekeeping book. This concern for perfection in his makeup was to result in the one tiny imperfection in an otherwise perfect crime. He had either to give up the idea of a perfectly kept expense account, or waste the price of a return trip. The truth is, moreover, that Landru lacked the modicum of imagination or sensitivity that would have allowed him to pursue peacefully an honorable craftsman's trade.

Even if there had only been this one detail to go by, we could not have compared Landru and Verdoux. A mania for keeping accounts argues a touch of meanness. The mind of Monsieur Verdoux is broader and freer. The perfect precision he brought to his crimes made it impossible to put a finger on him, but it did not rule out a touch of fantasy and of the spirit of adventure.

Besides, he played the stock exchange. No reckless entry in a cook's notebook would cost *him* his head—only a financial event of world-wide importance. Almost wiped out by the Wall Street crash and devaluation, reduced to the same conditions as our luckless small investors, but still able to keep his end up, even at the cost of some skimping, Verdoux decides one night that he has had enough. The police do not arrest him—he gives himself up, and in a short while we will see how and why.

It is easy to foresee what people will find to criticize in *Monsieur Verdoux*. There is a fairly complete list of them in an article in *La Revue des Temps Modernes* which goes about as far as anything could in misrepresentation. The author of the critique expresses herself as profoundly disappointed by Chaplin's work because to her it seems ideologically, psychologically, and aesthetically incoherent. "Monsieur Verdoux's crimes are dictated neither by a need for self-defense nor in order to repair injustices, nor by a deep ambition, nor by the desire to improve anything in the world around him. It is a sad thing to have expended so much energy and proved absolutely nothing, to have succeeded in producing neither a comedy nor a film with social implications, and to have beclouded the most important issues."

A remarkable misconstruction, thanks to which *Monsieur Verdoux* will remain a closed book to three-quarters of the public. For what have we here—a comedy or a film *à thèse?* Is its purpose to prove or even to explain anything? Marxists condemn Chaplin for his pessimism and for not clearly formulating the message they felt he owed them ever since the film *Modern Times.* Thus literary and political distortion join hands. Those in favor of a classical art with a psychological foundation find themselves in agreement with the political-minded while both are blind to the wonderful necessity of *Monsieur Verdoux*—that of *myth.*

The moment one includes Monsieur Verdoux in the Chaplin myth everything becomes clear, ordered, crystallized. Before any "character" and before the coherent, rounded-off life story that novelists and playwrights call fate, there exists a person called Charlie. He is a black-and-white form printed on the silver nitrate of film. This form is human enough to grip us and encourage our interest and sympathy. There is enough continuity of appearance and behavior about it to give its existence meaning and to attain to the autonomous existence of what is called, not without some ambiguity, "a character." I say ambiguity because the word applies equally to a character in a novel. But Charlie is not the Princesse de Clèves. Some day a decision must be made to rid Charlie and his progressive stages of development from those extravagant comparisons with the evolution of Molière by which people felt they could honor him. A character in a novel or a play works out his destiny within the confines of one work—we must not be misled by the saga novel which is, all things considered, only a matter of size. Charlie, on the other hand, always transcends the films in which he appears.

André Malraux recounts how, somewhere one Arabian night, he saw the most marvelous Chaplin film projected onto a white wall where sleeping cats lay: an odd serpent pieced out of second-hand strips of film picked up here and there. The myth was manifested there in its purest form.

It is Felix the Cat or Mickey Mouse rather than Molière's Misanthrope or Tartuffe who can throw light on the existence of Charlie. It is true that the cinema, like the comic strip, vaudeville, the circus, or the *commedia dell'arte,* has heroes standardized in appearance and possessing definite characteristics whom the public likes to see week by week in adventures which, for all their variety, are always those of the same person. However, I think we should avoid a too hasty and superficial comparison. We must first establish hierarchies in the degree and form of their existence. One cannot really speak of myth short of an understanding and development of characters. Charlie was a product of the Mack Sennett comedies, in which he had a smaller role than Fatty Arbuckle; but there was an exceptional depth to him, the appeal of a special kind of credibility, a consistency of behavior that owed nothing to psychology or to physical abnormality, a magical radiance in his glance differentiating him from the marionettes that surrounded him—and all of this foreshadowed a special destiny. In less than fifteen years, the little fellow with the ridiculous cutaway coat, the little trapezoid moustache, the cane, and the bowler hat, had become part of the consciousness of mankind. Never since the world began had a myth been so universally accepted.

I have no desire to undertake the exegesis of this myth, which would require a dismayingly large number of references ranging from the personal psychoanalysis of Charles Spencer Chaplin to universal symbolism, by way of Jewish mythology and various hypotheses about contemporary civilization. I doubt, with so short a historical perspective to go by, whether we can yet form a coherent and over-all view of Charlie. Condensed in him, as the psychoanalysts say, is too much sensitivity: too many collective unconsciousnesses are stored up inside him, providing opportunities for secret and powerful interassimilations, for formidable stratified mythological overlays, for archetypal upheavals, for mutations of meaning as yet beyond our grasp. But it is sufficient for my purpose to point out in Charlie a few constant factors, and also a few of the variants: to follow along paths taken by his character and to suggest, in the absence of a master key, three or four clues that are generally acceptable. I will be at pains above all not to lose sight of the fact that we are faced with a mythological process and to order my criticism accordingly.

If *Verdoux* has a "meaning," why look for it in terms of some moral, political, or social ideology or other, or even in reference to psychological categories that we are in the habit of seeing as revealed in the characters of our theater or our novels, when it is so easy to discover it in Charlie?

The critic quoted above attacks Chaplin's performance, accusing him of failing to escape altogether from the comic format of his former character, of hesitating, not choosing one way or another, between the realistic interpretation that the role of Verdoux demands and the conventions of a "Charlie." The fact is that in this instance realism would add up to illusion. Charlie is always there as if superimposed on Verdoux, because Verdoux *is* Charlie. It is important that at the right moment the public should recognize him without any shadow of a doubt; and this wonderful moment arrives in the final shot when Verdoux, alias Charlie, goes off in shirtsleeves between the executioners. Verdoux, or Charlie disguised as his opposite! There is no feature of the former character that is not turned inside out like the fingers of a glove. No ridiculous cutaway, no bowler, no outsize boots, no bamboo cane, rather a dapper suit, a broad, gray, silk tie, a soft felt hat, a gold-handled cane. The tiny trapezoid moustache, his supremely distinctive mark, has disappeared. The social positions of Charlie and Verdoux are radically different: Charlie, even when he is a millionaire, remains the eternal beggar; Verdoux is a rich man. When it is Charlie's moment to marry, it is always with dreadful termagants who terrorize him and squeeze the last penny of his pay out of him. The polygamous Verdoux is always unfaithful to his wives, forces them into submission, murders them, and lives off their money (except for the young woman in ill health and the one he decides not to poison—but we will deal with these exceptions later).

Furthermore, Charlie obviously has an inferiority complex *vis-à-vis* the opposite sex while Verdoux plays Don Juan and succeeds at it. The Charlie of *The Gold Rush* is soft-hearted and naïve; Verdoux is a cynic. No matter into how many elements you break Charlie down there is not one whose opposite you will not find in Verdoux.

Let us sum up all these characteristics in a single one. Charlie is essentially a socially unadapted person; Verdoux is superadapted. By reversing the character, the whole Chaplin universe is turned upside down at one stroke. The relations of Charlie with society (along with women, the fundamental and permanent theme of his work) have all switched their value. For example the police who terrorize Charlie are easily tricked by Verdoux. Far from running from the cops, Verdoux eludes them without having to stay out of their way, and when the game has gone on long enough and he decides to give himself up to one or more of them, it will be the police who are scared. But the scene is worth recounting. One night, Verdoux, aging and penniless, meets the young girl he had spared and even helped out of a difficult spot. Grateful to him and anxious on her part to do him a good turn, she takes him into a cabaret. She is now a rich woman, married to an arms manufacturer—a sweet man in spite of that, she says. Is it this final disappointment, is it weariness, or does he think that the time has arrived to put an end to it all? Verdoux pretends with friendly sincerity to accept the help offered him but after leaving the young woman he returns to the nightclub where, in passing, he had spotted the relatives of one of his victims. They have recognized him. He knows they have telephoned the police and that in a minute or two they will arrive. It would be easy to summon a taxi, but instead he returns calmly and finds himself face to face with the enemy, an old woman and her nephew. He does a quick feint and manages to lock them in an alcove near the cloakroom. The police arrive on the scene, a crowd starts to form in front of the locked door through which we can hear shouting. The police stand there open-mouthed, and alongside them is Verdoux, who could still escape without attracting attention. But no. He remains, curious and impassive. The door is forced open but there is naturally no murderer inside. The terrified old woman, half-fainting, comes to her senses—face to face with Verdoux. She faints away a second time, this time into Verdoux's arms while he, embarrassed, hands her to a cop. The scene is repeated several times until finally, overcoming her fright, the old lady manages to denounce him, indicating him with her finger. Paralyzed with astonishment, the incredulous policeman asks, "Could you be Monsieur Verdoux?" "At your service," he replies, giving a little bow. Before hastening to handcuff him, the representative of law and order wavers and hesitates, himself within an ace of fainting.

Let the reader put himself, for a moment, in the policeman's place. From the instant Charlie was born (yet how can you measure his existence by time?) society has directed its police force to drive him out of its bosom. The cops have been used to charging after him at street corners, on deserted wharfs, in public squares after closing time. His awkward and precipitous flight has always indicated a vague sense of self-confessed guilt, the condign punishment for which, moreover, is a blow from a truncheon. Actually this little fellow with the ducklike waddle gives them little trouble. His mischievousness and artfulness drive him to nothing more than harmless little acts of revenge or to the minimum of petty thefts necessary for survival. He was an easy victim who always eluded them at the last moment but always recognized his guilt. Then suddenly Charlie disappears! No more recognition of guilt! Now it is society that is inflicted with a strange uneasiness: not of course that it feels guilty, or at least it won't admit to being guilty (that we have never seen, for society by its nature can only accuse others.) But finally something abnormal is happening in its bosom which causes it to be far more disturbed than by the disorder that it ordinarily sanctions. The women who disappear, and this elusive character to whom, if he exists, these monstrous and incomprehensible crimes must be attributed, disturb its conscience as a society—not because it is unable to prevent and punish them, but chiefly because they are of such a kind that society vaguely senses their ambiguity. It reacts emotionally with a holy wrath, and this already indicates a troubled subconscious. Society knows it is guilty but cannot acknowledge the fact. When Monsieur Verdoux explains to the tribunal that all he has done is to apply, down to the last detail, the fundamental law of social relationships, the received wisdom of modern life that "business is business," society of course covers its face and cries scandal, and all the louder because the point has gone home. Its attack on Monsieur Verdoux will be all the more savage because it refuses to see in him a parody of society, an application *ad absurdum* of its rules of the game. Contrary to K in *The Trial* (and Charlie is not unrelated to him) Verdoux by his existence renders society guilty. It does not know what of exactly, but so long as this element of scandal survives in its bosom, the world will be sick and troubled. Unfortunately for society, Verdoux knows the game so well that he profits by it to remain out of reach. He can push audacity to the point of gazing in curiosity over the shoulder of the policeman who is looking for him. The fright of the poor official as he turns around is understandable.

Naturally society condemns Verdoux to death. In this way it hopes to be rid of the whole business, to wipe away totally the shocking stain on its existence. But it cannot see that, if Verdoux has deigned to hand himself over to justice, it is because the verdict can no longer touch him—better still, it will even deal itself a blow through him. From the moment of his arrest, Verdoux is totally indifferent to his fate. The limits of irony are passed when he is visited in prison by a journalist and a priest and asks the latter if there is anything he can do for him. All these final scenes are unspeakably beautiful, not so much from perfection of dramatic form but essentially because of the power of the situation and of the character itself. Verdoux presides over his last hours like a Socrates and, less talkative than Socrates, he holds society at bay by the mere fact of his presence. Society performs its final rite—the cigarette, the glass of rum, but Verdoux neither smokes nor drinks. He refuses this ill-timed offer with a mechanical gesture. Then follows one of Chaplin's most brilliant gags, a brain wave of genuis. He changes his mind. "I have never tasted rum!" he says, and with an air of curiosity he tastes it. The next instant there shines through Verdoux's fugitive and bright glance, the awareness of death. Not fear, or courage, or resignation—certainly this elementary psychology comes into play—but something like a passivity of will which combines all the gravity of the moment with something that transcends indifference, contempt, even the certainty of revenge. He alone has known for a long time what lay ahead for society. He does not interfere with it. Now all has been accomplished.

We see Verdoux next being led away across the prison yard in the dawn, between two executioners. A small man in his shirt sleeves, his arms tied behind him, he moves forward toward the scaffold with a kind of a hop, skip, and a jump. Then comes the sublimest gag of all, unspoken but unmistakable, the gag that resolves the whole film: Verdoux was Charlie! *They're going to guillotine Charlie!* The fools did not recognize him. In order to force society to commit this irreparable blunder, Charlie has decked out the simulacrum of his opposite. In the precise and mythological meaning of the word, Verdoux is just an avatar of Charlie —the chief and we may indeed say the first. As a result *Monieur Verdoux* is undoubtedly the most important of Chaplin's works. When we see it, we are seeing the first evolution of a step which could well be, by the same token, the final step. *Monsieur Verdoux* casts a new light on Chaplin's world, sets it right and gives it a new significance. This same road to nowhere, always taken from film to film by the little fellow with the cane, which some see as the road of the wandering Jew while others prefer to identify it with the road of hope—now we know where it ends. It ends as a path across a prison yard in the morning mist, through which we sense the ridiculous shape of a guillotine.

Let there be no mistake, the scandal created by the film in the United States could well take as a pretext the obvious immorality of the character. The truth is that society reacted to it: it sensed something implacable, like a menace, in the serenity of Verdoux's death. It guessed, to tell the whole truth, that Charlie at one and the same time was triumphant over it and escaped its clutches, that he has put society forever in the wrong; for it is not enough to say that the road ends in the scaffold: through one of his most beautiful ellipses, Chaplin avoided showing us the finale. The blade of the guillotine will only cut up an apparition. We seem to guess at the existence of a double of the executed man: dressed in a white tunic, decked out with the fluffy paper wings he wore in the dream sequence of *The Kid,* Charlie escapes by superimposition, unknown to the executioners. Even before the ludicrous deed is accomplished, Charlie is in heaven.

I amuse myself imagining Charlie's final avatar, his ultimate adventure: the settling of his account with St. Peter—even if I were God the Father, I would not feel at ease welcoming Monsieur Verdoux.

Monsieur Verdoux is Chaplin's New Testament. The Old ended with *The Gold Rush* and *The Circus.* Between the two, the Chaplin myth seems to be confused, troubled, uncertain. He is still trying to rely on gags and comic bits which, however, grow fewer and fewer. *The Great Dictator* is significant from this point of view. Although badly constructed, mixed up, oddly assorted, it did have one brilliant and fortuitous justification, a settling of accounts with Hitler, who well deserved it, for his two-fold impudence of stealing Charlie's moustache and of raising himself to the rank of the gods. In obliging Hitler's moustache to become again part of the Charlie myth, Charlie wiped out the myth of the dictator. The film had to be made, even if only for the sake of our mental satisfaction and of the due ordering of things, but it was a chance variant in the avatars of the hero. Besides, we clearly see a disintegration of the character in *The Great Dictator,* especially in one scene, at once the worst dramatically and in its conformity with the phenomenology of the myth the most beautiful: I refer to the final speech. In this interminable, yet (in my view) too short scene I remember only the spellbinding tone of a voice and the most disconcerting of metamorphoses. Charlie's lunar mask disappears little by little, corroded by the gradations of the panchromatic stock and betrayed by the nearness of the camera, which intensifies the telescopic effect of the wide screen. Underneath, as if it were a superimposition, appears the face of an already aging man, furrowed here and there by grief, his hair sprinkled with white, the face of Charles Spencer Chaplin. The photographic psychoanalysis of Charlie, as it were, remains certainly one of the great moments in world cinema.

All the same, and indeed by its very beauty, it reveals an unhealthy condition of the myth, a pernicious infection of the character, which, if it continued, could not but destroy it utterly. Indeed, one might have expected, with some likelihood, to find nothing more in *Monsieur Verdoux* than the actor (prodigious undoubtedly, but still the actor) Charles S. Chaplin. Nothing of the sort, it was just that sickly condition which precedes moulting and the shedding of skins. Charlie was getting ready to shed his skin. Like Jupiter planning one of his naughty escapades here on earth, he was to return to us unrecognizable and beget on society one of those children she would remember.

What is admirable about Monsieur Verdoux is that his activities have a much deeper significance than those of Charlie in *The Gold Rush* although they are of a completely opposite kind. Actually, from the first Keystone shorts to *The Gold Rush* and *The Circus* Charlie's character has passed through a moral and psychological evolution. The initial Charlie is rather naughty, kicking out right and left at the backsides of his rivals as soon as they are no longer in a position to retaliate.

In *Kid Auto Races at Venice* we see him bite the nose of an inquisitive bystander without the slightest warning. The character gradually improves but it is touch and go for a long while. Before the maternal instinct he reveals in *The Kid* (and it is only after he has done his best to get rid of him, that he decides to adopt the little Jackie Coogan) he has shown little sympathy for children. In *A Day's Pleasure,* taking advantage of the absence of witnesses, one of those little backward kicks that are his specialty sends flying the mint lozenges and the acid drops that the ship's bellboy offers him. Besides, it is a regular rule of conduct with him not to hesitate to do some mean little thing when no one is looking.

He shams easily and is tricky to no good purpose. It would be wrong to think that Charlie is basically good. Only love makes him so, and then there are no limits to his generosity and courage. In *Easy Street* and even in *The Pilgrim* we find more than one example of his naughtiness. However, these faults of his do not detract from our interest in the character or from our sympathy. In fact, the opposite is true. These words must be dissociated from any implied moral judgment. Being on the side of the hero of a myth, the fact that we are both for and with him, fortunately is not uniquely dependent on the moral categories of which he may be the embodiment. But it is a law common to the evolution of all characters that live by virtue of intercourse with the public, that they tend to justify our sympathy for them by greater psychological consistency and greater moral perfection. The character of Pierrot follows the same curve. Thus it is that in *The Gold Rush* Charlie has become completely good. His misfortunes never come under the stricture of moral condemnation. On the contrary, they make a victim out of him and stir us on occasions to something beyond sympathy, namely to pity. Here Charlie is at the end of a process of evolution that justifies our coming to the conclusion that it does not represent his work at its best. As far as I am concerned, I would rather have the rich equivocation of *The Pilgrim* in which his art has not yet troubled about, or become enfeebled by, a concern for psychological and moral values. In any event, *The Gold Rush* is the most forceful apology for the character and most clearly calls for us to revolt against Charlie's fate.

The Saint Verdoux of today is the dialectical answer to Saint Charlie of *The Kid, The Circus,* and *The Gold Rush.* But in my view the indictment of Charlie's enemies and the vindication provided by the character are all the more convincing because they are not based on any psychological proof. We go along with Verdoux, we are *for* Verdoux. But how can our sympathy be based on our moral estimate of him? On that level the spectator too could only condemn Verdoux's cynicism. Yet we take him as he is. It is the character that we love, not his qualities or his defects. The audience's sympathy for Verdoux is focused on the myth, not on what he stands for morally. So when Verdoux, with the spectator on his side, is condemned by society, he is doubly sure of victory because the spectator condemns the condemnation of a man "justly" condemned by society. Society no longer has any emotional claim on the public conscience.

Monsieur Verdoux is at once a paradox and a *tour de force*. *The Gold Rush* went straight for its goal. Verdoux takes society in the rear like a boomerang; his triumph is in no way indebted to the ready and dubious help of ethics. The myth is self-sufficient, it convinces by its own inner logic. There are some theorems in geometry whose truth is only finally established when their opposites have been proved. *Monsieur Verdoux* is needed to fill out and round off Chaplin's work. Between the timid and unhappy lover of *The Gold Rush* and this Don Juan past his prime, society is completely caught up in the dialectic of the myth. The reflex action with which it imprudently tried to get rid of the myth released the final spring of the trap. Feeling morally and legally justified in condemning Bluebeard to death while it had been satisfied only to jail the naïve striker of *Modern Times,* lo and behold society killed *Charlie*!

It now remains to be explained precisely why Chaplin chose for his daring act of defiance against society an assault on women. I have reserved until now this aspect of the myth which I consider to be more personal and biographical.

To begin with, this polygamous speculator harbors a touching secret: he has a wife, a child, a hearth and home. It is in large part to supply their needs and to keep them in quiet comfort that he is forever, up hill and down dale, in the process of poisoning someone. His wife, his first and only one, has become an invalid. She is frail and gentle. We learn, at the end of the film, from the mouth of the aged Verdoux, just before he surrenders to the police, that she and the child are dead. Naturally we have no proof that he didn't poison them. From the way he adds that they are certainly "happier up above," we might even think he did. At bottom how differently could he have treated this wife whom he loved than by killing her for love rather than for her money as he did the others? Verdoux has no prejudices about death; he knows what's good about it and doesn't hesitate to choose it when that's the wise thing to do. It may be that, financially ruined, weary of the struggle and no longer able to assure a peaceful existence for the one he loved, or perhaps knowing that her suffering was incurable, he had gently spared her the propinquity of a world against which he could no longer defend her.

The second exception is a young women he met in the street and brought home one night to try out a new poison he had just concocted. The young woman, believing him a good man, confides her misfortunes to him. She wants to come to the help of the man she loves. She believes in life because she believes in this man's love. She is battling despair with all her might so as to save him. Touched, Verdoux exchanges the poison for a glass of burgundy, and presses two thousand-franc notes into the unhappy girl's hand. When, at the end of the film, he comes across her a second time, she might have been of more effective help to him. It is not so much material help that Verdoux now needs—it is not even love. Tenderness, affection, would be enough. But he must also be able to believe in the happiness of this woman whose husband, who makes her so happy, is after all, he now learns, just a munitions maker like the rest of them. If that night he had met only one just person, a single woman who really deserved her happiness, perhaps he would have done society a favor and decided not to surrender himself into the hands of its justice.

Even under the guise of Verdoux-Bluebeard, Charlie follows and perfects his personal myth of the woman whom we may here call (in remembrance of her first embodiment) the Edna Purviance complex. At this point I will put forward a hypothesis which does not claim to be all inclusive but which seems at least to explain some aspects of the character of Verdoux in its relation both to Charlie and to Chaplin. There is no need to have recourse to the latest subtleties of psychoanalysis to see quite evidently that Chaplin, by way of Charlie, pursues symbolically one and the same feminine myth. Between the tender and gentle Edna Purviance, the blind girl of *City Lights,* and Verdoux's frail invalid there is no noticeable difference except that Verdoux is married to the last named. Like Charlie, they are all unhappy human beings, ill adjusted to society, physical or moral invalids of social life. It is this hyperfemininity which beguiles

Charlie; love's lightning stroke is the cause of a shattering conversion to the norms of society and morality. At the beginning of *Easy Street,* naturally it is not the pastor's sermon but his daughter's smile that transforms the miscreant into an instrument of virtue. There is one exception to the rule: *The Kid* in which pseudo-paternal love takes the place of love for a pure young girl. If we correctly interpret the symbolism of these female characters then the whole of Charlie's work would be the ever-renewed search for the woman capable of reconciling him to society and by the same token to himself. The public, remembering only Charlie's kindness and goodness, remembers only a Charlie in love. They forget that the winnings he offers to the young immigrant girl were gained by cheating during the game. In *Modern Times* Charlie dreams of living an honest and industrious life in which he returns in the evening to his petty-bourgeois house with a good feeling of a day well spent, and finds the little woman he loves busy getting dinner ready. Love alone can prompt his desire, albeit blundering and comic for other reasons, not only to adapt himself to society but one might even say to accept a moral way of living and a psychological individualism. For the sake of Edna Purviance Charlie feels capable of assuming a character and a destiny: the myth becomes a man.

In relation to this combination of events, found in almost all Charlie movies, Verdoux represents likewise an important development. Depending on the case, a film may end, as in *The Pilgrim,* with the collapse of the idyll, or, as in *The Gold Rush* or *The Immigrant,* with marriage. The fact is, though, that the upbeat dénouement should not be taken seriously. It is brought about—and on this point a comparison with Molière is possible—by a dramatic reflex that is foreign to the myth. The true ending, which the audience unconsciously reconstructs, is that of *Sunnyside* or of *Modern Times;* though again one might consider this absence of a dénouement to be an optimistic development of the undeniable failures of love in *The Pilgrim* or *The Circus.*

For the first time in Monsieur Verdoux, we see Charlie after his marriage to Edna Purviance. Maybe because he has rounded the cape of love that, at least according to the logic of the myth, Charlie can change him-

115

self into Verdoux, or perhaps, if you prefer, Verdoux simply had to be married to Edna Purviance. In any case, although he is not all that reconciled to society, he at least knows how to make use of it. We also know, and this is important, that he continues to respect the wife-child myth but no longer hopes to be saved by it. Maybe, supposing we accept the murder theory, he respects the myth even to the point of poisoning Edna Purviance to prevent her from becoming the responsibility of life and society.

The second young woman to be spared might conceivably represent a more vital Edna Purviance, who refuses to die. But without knowing it, she crosses over into the opposite camp.

We are now left with those other women, the ones who can be poisoned, and also those who resist on occasion—for the most important character in the film is precisely the woman Verdoux does not manage to kill. Chaplin, whom one can criticize after his recent films for his increasing fear of talented actors, has made a fortunate choice here in Martha Raye, the unspeakably comic termagant, the clinging woman of so many American comedies. By asking a well-known actress, one already established in a continuing role, to play opposite him, Charlie whether he knew it or not wanted to set a character rather than an actor over against Verdoux. Hollywood's number-one pain in the neck, the nagging Martha Raye, who could make wild beasts out of lambs and justify the acquittal of a dozen Bluebeards, is precisely the one indestructible woman whose capacity for resistance Verdoux cannot overcome. I am impressed by the fact that Chaplin did not hesitate to seize on a mythology foreign to his own and used a character that up to this point owed nothing to him, but who will henceforth owe him everything.

It is Martha Raye who vindicates Verdoux in the viewer's mind. The one murder that Chaplin deals with at length (and cleverly too) is that of a harridan—and what's more, he fluffs it. The whole middle part of the film is taken up by one gag of formidable dimensions, and droll beyond words: the poisoning that didn't come off. The others are handled so artfully in line with the Chaplin technique that our sensibilities, skillfully manipulated, feel no sense of repugnance over Verdoux's activities. It is Bluebeard, instead, for whom one feels sorry. Thus he manages to have his revenge on women without having to sacrifice his splendid role of victim.

For here it is also doubtless a question of revenge. While *Monsieur Verdoux* extends and goes beyond the myth, hitherto incomplete, of pure love for Edna Purviance, Chaplin gives Verdoux the task of revenging him on the other women. It might well be true to say that Charlie's feminine ideal is more or less consciously Chaplin's own. I would be ready to see clear indications of this in his use of these new loves of his, succeeding Edna Purviance in the embodiment of the myth. But in private life reality customarily gives the lie to mythological idealization. Objectively speaking, the faults of the woman or of Chaplin himself are of little importance here. It is reasonable to assume that they are there simply to justify consciously a divorce which was unconsciously inevitable from the beginning of the idyll. If it is the female myth not the woman that Chaplin is in search of, then no single woman can satisfy him, and his disappointment is all the keener in proportion as the "crystallization" of his initial feeling has caused him subjectively to identify his new love with the ideal. "The thirteenth woman returns as the first."

The discarded wife is not just a wife one no longer loves—she is expelled from the myth. For Chaplin-Charlie (Charlie being here Chaplin's unconscious) she has betrayed the Edna Purviance whom Chaplin saw in her. Thus all women are guilty save one—who will join the others later. The myth of Don Juan is merged with that of Bluebeard. One may consider Verdoux's murder victims to be symbols of Chaplin's former wives, who were likewise his wives on the screen. Not to mention that Chaplin symbolically recoups, through Monsieur Verdoux, the alimony extorted from him with the complicity of American society and the law by various "Edna Purviances" who turned into "Martha Rayes" after divorcing him.

For it was public opinion that first took upon itself to make a Bluebeard out of Chaplin, even before he created *Monsieur Verdoux*. The author of *A Woman of Paris* (known in French as *L'Opinion publique*) was content to face up to the myth in which he was already imprisoned, freeing himself from it by fulfilling it and justifying it symbolically. The misogyny of Chaplin finds in Verdoux both the judge and the executioner of women. But they deserve to die because all, to one degree or another, are guilty of betraying the hope embodied in Edna Purviance.

What could be the meaning of the formal aesthetic problems of the narrative and the direction if, as I have tried to show, the reality of the work resides in the symbolism of the situation and the characters? It's clear that we cannot here apply the usual criteria of cinematic dramaturgy. Obviously Chaplin does not build the substance of his narrative on the basis of a skeletal scenario, of an abstract dramatic structure, even the very substantial one of tragedy. It is this that may set one on the wrong track or deceive one in analyzing his films. They are only sequences of quasi-autonomous scenes, each of which is content to exploit a situation to the full. Think back to what you can remember of Charlie, and dozens of scenes will come to mind as clear cut as the picture of the character himself; but whether we are dealing with the gas lamp in *Easy Street,* the sermon on David and Goliath, the papier-maché tree in *Shoulder Arms,* the dance of the rolls, Charlie's capers when he is being beaten up on the sidewalk in *The Great Dictator,* the dream in *The Kid,* or twenty other scenes, all are sufficient unto themselves, smooth and round like an egg, so that one might almost extrapolate them from one film to another. Certainly it would be a mistake to put all of Chaplin's work on the same level. The dramatic progression of *The Pilgrim,* for example, is admirable, that of *Easy Street* enchantingly clear, but *Shoulder Arms* is divided into three distinct parts which constitute, dramatically, independent films. Even in the best-made of his films the so-called structural qualities are the most extrinsic to them, the last by which we would determine their excellence. Of course it would have been better if Chaplin had known how to reconcile the dramatic development of a story with the development of the situations of which it is composed, even better still, if this useful ordering of succession and interrelation conveyed a more hidden order in the conceiving and developing of a gag, and, most of all, that mysterious economy which gives the scenes, however short, their spiritual density, their specific gravity as myth and as comedy. The only serious formal criticisms that can be leveled against a Chaplin film concern its unity of style, the unfortunate variations in tone, the conflicts in the symbolism implicit in the situations. From this point of view the quality of Chaplin's films since *The Gold Rush* has definitely fallen off. Despite some first-rate scenes, even *Modern Times* suffers from an evident lack of unity between gags. *

As for *The Great Dictator,* it is a collection of uneven scenes; some of them, like the one with the artillery shell, might even pass for mediocre reminders of the Keystone days. The grenade gag could have fitted right into *Shoulder Arms.* I don't think much of the meeting between the two dictators, which introduces a tired old custard-pie routine into a work that contains scenes of sheer dramatic tension such as the one in which Charlie sits and watches his house burn down. In this scene, as Jean-Louis Barrault has said, the mime of despair, the choreography of anguish, find their most perfect expression in immobility.

As a rule, this falling off in quality in Chaplin's next to last films is attributed to a parasitic ideology. As we know, Chaplin has some pretensions to being a social philosopher, and no injustice is done to the artist to find his ideas, though appealing, also an encumbrance. Clearly *Easy Street,* or for that matter *The Gold Rush,* do not set out to prove anything, while there is no mistaking the purpose or theses of *Modern Times, The Great Dictator,* and *Monsieur Verdoux.* We could willingly do without these; but it remains to determine if they are as important as has been alleged. In proportion as any "message" animates a character, to that extent it displaces the myth and tends to displace the character too. The ontology of the hero is destroyed. But thank God this destruction does not follow as inevitably as one might suppose. The myth resists; harassed and constrained by Chaplin's ideas, it finds in the genius of Chaplin himself a

---

* The commercial reissue of *Modern Times* has given me an opportunity to quash this judgment, which was based on memory. Today, indeed, I am almost ready to claim *Modern Times* as one of the best of Charlie's full-length films—perhaps the best, along with *City Lights.*

So far from lacking unity, *Modern Times* on the contrary is the film in which the level of acting style is best maintained, controlling thus the style of the gags and even of the script. The ideological significance never impinges from without on the comic flow of the gags. It is the imperturbable logic of the latter that utterly exposed the absurdities of our society.

way to escape from them, and to reappear elsewhere, perhaps even without Chaplin being aware of it. But the symbolism of the character is more complicated; we have to separate it from the relations between the character and the situation, and also from the relation between the character and the message. Almost every gesture, an unexpected sign of some sort, informs us that Charlie is at last ready to treat the idea itself as a prop, an object of some sort to be introduced into the performance. The globe in *The Great Dictator* is a good example: a symbol of an idea of the most general kind, it becomes a choreographic prop in the development of a scene where we return to Charlie's 1916 sense of the comic. It is his way of juggling with ideas even when they are the ideas of citizen Chaplin.

But *Monsieur Verdoux* does not even need any such justification as that provided by the group of arguments I am presuming to offer in defense of the "accused." It is difficult to know what Chaplin's ideological intentions were in conceiving this film but they have in no sense interfered with the character since his behavior in the situations in which he finds himself is thoroughly autonomous, coherent, and meaningful. Hence it would be more correct to blame this on the weakening of the myth since the making of *The Gold Rush* rather than the proliferation of parasitic ideology in the scenarios of Charles Spencer Chaplin. It would be senseless to imagine and to hope retrospectively for a prolongation of the Charlie character, arbitrarily established at a level which we happen to believe to be a satisfactory stage of its evolution. The hero created by Chaplin was dependent on many factors, as various as they were decisive. The transition from orthochromatic stock to panchromatic should itself alone have brought on a veritable morphological disorder, more serious perhaps than even the introduction of the spoken word: acknowledging and revealing that the actor was aging, it ate away at the character. Try and imagine Charlie in Technicolor! But we must also take into consideration the general history of the cinema, its technical evolution, the increasing sensitivity of the public, and, above all, Charlie's own life story, which we have taken to be not unconnected with the mythology of his character. On the contrary, one might be delighted at the metamorphosis of Charlie into Verdoux so long as the latter fits in with the rebirth of a myth able to secrete anew its ideological antitoxins.

So far from being badly put together, *Monsieur Verdoux* strikes me as one of Chaplin's best-made films, thanks to the new-found vigor of the character, to the homogeneity of the myth. Jean Renoir made no mistake. He was doubtless the only person in Hollywood able to appreciate its structure, completely built from within, a thoroughly workmanlike job. Renoir himself has never been able to "construct" a scenario and for basically the same reasons. Renoir has always been more concerned with the creation of characters and situations in which they could express themselves rather than with a story. There is also a Renoir mythology—obviously more diffused and spread out over many more characters—as *La Règle du jeu* clearly shows: the only reason for the bearskin was to provide the author-actor with an opportunity to achieve the metempsychosis of which he dreamed. Let the scenarios cope with the bearskins! I have no wish to push the comparison too far, since this could falsify the meaning of Renoir's work, into which quite other aesthetic contradictions enter. Yet it remains true that the director of *La Partie de campagne* likewise has always tried to direct *the* film in which the narrative would flow from the characters in a given situation. Each scene in *La Règle du jeu* is resolved on its own terms. We feel that it presented itself to the director as a special case. He treats it like an autonomous organism, as the gardener treats his rose bush. It gives me great pleasure to find a garden and roses in both *Monsieur Verdoux* and *Diary of a Chambermaid*. These images are not accidental, for Renoir lights up his film with the same cheerful cruelty.

We must not conclude, therefore, that Chaplin's film has no formal structure, no narrative architecture, and that the direction consists in nothing more than setting up situations. Just the opposite, in fact. To recall what film direction owes not only to *A Woman of Paris* but to Charlie's work as a whole is to repeat a truism. *Monsieur Verdoux* shows its originality precisely in achieving a kind of synthesis between the celebrated psychological film directed by Chaplin and the films in which Charlie appears. Whereby we clearly see that the technique of ellipsis and allusion which was the definitive aesthetic revelation of *A Woman of Paris* somehow naturally befits the character. Chaplin's method of direction consists in carrying Charlie's performance over into the camerawork, the shooting script, and the editing. But Chaplin's ellipsis, whether applied to space or time, is not really concerned with what we call the scenario. It only affects the narrative at the scene level in immediate relation to the actor within the structure of the situation. It would be impossible to think of a closer dependence of content and form, or, better, a more perfect fusion of the two. Ellipsis gives definition to the aesthetic crystallization of Chaplin's work. But in this connection, *Monsieur Verdoux* is undoubtedly the most completely crystallized film of all. Although one can complain that the majority of the Charlie films are a succession of more or less perfect but relatively disordered scenes, the "cleavage planes" within *Monsieur Verdoux* are in some way homothetic to the much smaller units of ellipsis. Their interdependence is much more apparent than real. These dramatic crystals, when you bring them together, fit into one another. As we know, *Monsieur Verdoux* contains some of Chaplin's most perfect ellipses. I already mentioned the one of the guillotine we do not see. We are familiar with the furnace and its black smoke in the rose garden, or the killing of the woman indicated just by Verdoux's going into and coming out of the bridal chamber. But these ellipses scaled to actor and scene have their counterparts in the enormous gaps separating the sequences. To go from one to the other by way of an explanatory title indicating the year and the place where the next action unfolds is just a pseudo-awkwardness as normal in a plot of this kind as a little placard indicating the setting in the Shakespearean theater. As for the train shot which introduces various sequences and provides the film with an interior rhythm like a leitmotif, it reaches a level almost of abstraction, so tightly does it condense time and events into a single image.

What could mislead us about the formal qualities of *Monsieur Verdoux* and make us consider it less well made than, for example, *The Gold Rush* (whereas it is certainly more perfectly made) is a natural confusion in the spectator between the comic density of the film and the myth. Whenever one thinks of Charlie, he is inseparable from the comic routines with which he won over the public. Since *The Gold Rush,* there has been a sharp decline in the wealth of Chaplin's comic imagination. There is more inventiveness, there are more gags in three hundred feet of *The Pilgrim* than in all of his last four films. There is certainly no room here for congratulation. On the other hand, neither should we harbor any resentment against Chaplin, nor interpret the fact as necessarily indicating an aesthetic impoverishment. Rather, everything takes place in *Monsieur Verdoux* as if this undeniable draining of his comic genius was the price to be paid for, or perhaps the cause of, an increased refinement of the myth. The middle part of *Monsieur Verdoux* is lightened by a monstrous gag, the sturdy comic bulk of which testifies, to our delight, that it belongs to the geological strata of the good old Charlie films; but the business with the glass of rum, and especially the final image of the film, have a quality, a finesse, a purity, which is only found three or four times in all of Chaplin's work. I don't think one has to ask oneself if this collapse or erosion of Chaplin's comic genius is compensated for by an enriching of the myth. We have here two aesthetic values, incomparable in their richness. I think it is wiser to presume the existence here of some mysterious aesthetic necessity and (since I have plunged into geographical metaphors) to see in *Monseur Verdoux* the work nearest to that equilibrium profile in which the myth, like a river flowing effortlessly and without hindrance to the sea, deposits no more than a fine carpet of silt and of gold dust.

LIMELIGHT, OR THE DEATH OF MOLIÈRE

TO WRITE about *Limelight* is a task which has nothing in common with the professional critic's monotonous day-to-day, week-to-week job. The following comments, then, are a meditation upon an event called *Limelight*.

I am discussing the film before seeing it again in a public cinema. I write on the basis of the remarkable gathering at Biarritz at which the whole French cinema world wept at the sight of the death of Molière— that is to say, of Calvero, alias Chaplin. When I say wept, I am not exaggerating. As the lights went up, they revealed four hundred directors, screenwriters, and critics choked with emotion, their eyes red as tomatoes. There is only one word to describe the note struck by this film, and we must first restore it to its full classical meaning—sublime.

This performance was undoubtedly intended simply as a prepreview of *Limelight*. But the selectness of the spectators, and above all the presence of Chaplin, made of it a complex affair of which the film itself was just one component. The audience was at once the most alert and the most receptive ever assembled. Its predisposition to be favorable was conjoined with the greatest lucidity. But at the same time this unusual assembly was justified as much on the ground of Chaplin's presence as by the film itself. Half of the performance we attended was in the hall.

Granted, there is nothing so very original in such a situation, but what happened showed that in the circumstances it took on a very special significance. Naturally it was a matter of paying a moving tribute to Charles Chaplin—and much could be said about the enthusiasm aroused by his visit, and about the undiminished strength of his popularity. But this would not be enough to explain either the intensity or the quality of our emotional response to the film. I am going to try to make myself understood by setting up a ridiculous hypothesis: what would *Limelight* mean to an imaginary spectator who had never heard of Chaplin or of Charlie? Probably the question is meaningless because it contains a contradiction in terms—and this contradiction immediately gives us the measure of the film. There are certainly more people on earth who have never heard of Napoleon or Hitler or Churchill or Stalin, than of Charlie. *The Great Dictator* was not possible, indeed had no meaning, except insofar as Chaplin was sure that the myth of Charlie was more powerful and more real than that of Hitler, that their physical resemblance worked in his favor, and that Charlie would thereby drain his double of his blood, leaving only skin and bone. For it is crucial to grasp that the basis of the film was not the exploitation by Chaplin of his likeness to the man of Berchtesgaden; on the contrary, it was based on the unwitting imitation of Charlie by Hitler. To unmask the dictator, Chaplin had only to remind the world of his copyright in the moustache.

This is something that must be thoroughly understood before one starts thinking about *Limelight*. It is impossible to separate the story of Calvero from the Chaplin myth. I do not mean in the elementary and primary sense that one can discern in the story some obvious autobiographical elements—"a portrait of the artist by himself," as one English critic put it; but in a more basic sense, namely of a self-criticism of the myth by its author. *Verdoux* was already meant to do this: the killer of widows was Charlie disguised as his social opposite number. In *Limelight* the machinery is much more complex, to the decisive degree that we are not concerned with Charlie but with Chaplin himself. Verdoux, in a sense, represented the dialectical triumph of the character of Charlie and by the same token the end of him. *Limelight* treats by implication the relations between an actor and character he plays. Calvero was once famous but old age, helped on by alcoholism, lost him his engagements. In a few years

125

the public had virtually forgotten not only Calvero's name but even what he looked like, so that when he was offered a modest opportunity to return to the stage, he preferred to use a false name. This was a mistake, because the public might have paid some slight attention to Calvero, but was totally uninterested in an unknown, aging clown.

May we not see in this episode, as in Calvero's decision to give up the music hall in exchange for the anonymity of a street singer, a touching self-questioning on Chaplin's part? What would he be without the glory of being Charlie, what would he be, deprived of his myth and left to the resources of his craft with such strength as old age can muster?

Limelight, then, is certainly autobiography, above all in reverse. The downfall of Calvero, the heartlessness of the public, the renunciation of love by the old clown, are the shadows thrown behind Chaplin by the light of his glory, of his success, both professionally and in love. A psychoanalyst might go a step further and point out that to evoke this imaginary failure is not unconnected here with the failure of Chaplin's father, a singer who lost his voice and vainly sought consolation in drink. The London of the film is the London of Chaplin's wretched childhood, but the street urchins in *Limelight* are his own children, and in real life Calvero's rival in love is Sydney Chaplin.

But enough! A psychoanalysis of *Limelight* adds nothing to its value. All that matters is to reveal how intimately the work depends on its author. Futhermore, this dependence is not so much psychological as what we might call ontological. While *Limelight* is a direct evocation of Chaplin's childhood, this evocation is subordinated to the theme of the actor's relation with the character he plays. The true subject of the film remains: Can Charlie die? Can Charlie grow old? Instead of handling this two-fold and touching inquiry like a question to be answered, Chaplin exorcises it through a story of the lost fame and old age of a man who resembles him like a brother.

That night at Biarritz found us in a marvellously effective combination of circumstances. The audience was composed of the four hundred people in all of France to whom the myth of Charlie meant most—and Chaplin was there! Thus an extraordinary drama was enacted, with three characters: the audience, the film, and Chaplin. When I alluded above to the death of Molière, it was no exaggeration. Molière died on the stage like Calvero, playing in a farce in which he tried to exorcise sickness and death by making fun of doctors.

Thus we were in Chaplin's presence at the spectacle of his death. And we wept with all the more emotion because we knew he was present and alive. Our tears were multiplied by the gratitude we felt, by the joy that we anticipated when the lights went up of seeing once more his silvery hair, his smile touched with emotion, his blue eyes. Indeed he was there. The film was just a sublime bad dream, but a dream as true as reality, one that allowed us to measure our love for him in his most beautiful role: the death of a clown called Charlie. Who in the world since theater began, what playwright or actor, has ever reached that supreme and paradoxical position in his art of being in himself the object of his tragedy? Doubtless many authors have put themselves more or less into their works, but without the knowledge of the public and hence without the elements of drama. *Limelight* is not *Le Misanthrope,* nor is it a play *à clef,* and Chaplin is not Sacha Guitry. We are concerned with something other than his fame—his myth. Only the age of cinema, doubtless, allows the actor and his character to merge to this extent: Oedipus and Sophocles; Goethe and Faust; Cervantes and Don Quixote.

Molière died unobtrusively, surrounded by a few friends, and was buried by torchlight. Blessed be the cinema which frees our Molière from the necessity of dying in order to make of his death the most beautiful of all his films.

THE GRANDEUR OF *LIMELIGHT*

SOME PEOPLE may well have felt intimidated, in reacting to *Limelight,* by the critical terrorism that surrounded the first appearance of the film in Paris. There was no such favorable predisposition toward *Monsieur Verdoux* and no one was shocked by a divided press—nor by a divided public which had not exactly lined up for it. But then Chaplin had not come to play the traveling salesman for *Monsieur Verdoux.* His presence on this occasion created a strangely ambiguous situation. The wave of sympathy and curiosity stirred up by the person of the author broke over the film. To have any reservations about it was to set a limit to one's admiration for its maker. This confusion reached its height on the occasion of the historic showing at which Chaplin presented *Limelight* to the French film press and film makers—a paradoxical apotheosis at which the author offered his audience the dramatic spectacle of his own downfall and death. Through the power of the cinema the death of Molière became the fourth act of *Le Malade imaginaire.* When the lights went up, the entire audience, in tears, turned toward that same face that had just faded from the screen and sat stunned, as if at the end of a marvelous and terrible dream, to find him still alive. We could no longer distinguish between the admiration we felt for Chaplin and our sense of relief at being released, thanks to his presence, from a delicious fear.

And truly it seemed at first that these were parasitic emotions, not belonging to the work itself. Probably more than one among all those who expressed themselves in superlatives over *Limelight* would have been bored if they had not been influenced by public opinion. Some critics, or for that matter a lot of spectators, who were a little more sensitive than the rest, had mixed feelings about the film. They had enjoyed this or that aspect of it, but not the whole thing. They were annoyed at the moral pressure, at the blackmail asking for total admiration, that was seemingly being practiced on them. Basically, they were right. Nonetheless, I would like to defend the remarkable atmosphere of snobbism which surrounded the premiere of *Limelight*.

Undoubtedly Chaplin came to Europe to insure the proper launching of his film. *Monsieur Verdoux,* boycotted in the United States and coolly received in Europe, had been a commercial failure. Although *Limelight* had been made in a much shorter time—actually just a few weeks—it is reasonable to think that its success was of vital concern to its author-producer. He was right in thinking that the best possible publicity would be for him to be present. What happened seems to have borne him out. *Limelight* had an exceptional run but it was not a resounding success. The distributor had trouble fulfilling the minimum attendence of half a million admissions required by his contract—an enormous figure but one that those handling the exhibition felt would be easily reached. If it had not been for the extraordinary publicity the press gave Chaplin's visit and the sympathetic buildup this created for the film, the odds are strong that it would have been a resounding flop, even allowing for its importance.

There would have been nothing astonishing about this. It was easy at the outset to see how much in *Limelight* would disturb people who had gone in the anticipation of seeing "a Charlie Chaplin film"—which retained, even more than *Monsieur Verdoux,* some element of comedy. Nor was the melodramatic aspect of the story calculated to please people, because it was based on illusion. *Limelight* is a pseudo melodrama. Where melodrama is primarily defined by the absence of ambiguity in the characters, here Calvero is ambiguity itself; and whereas, from a dramatic point of view, melodrama requires that one should be able to forsee the outcome of the plot, *Limelight* is precisely a film in which what happens is never exactly what one might expect—its scenario is brim full of inventiveness as any ever written.

But the general public likes nothing better than to believe in a melo-drama that is frankly one—parodies prove this. Only a minimum of camou-flage is required so that the little housemaid in the balcony can feel that it is a proof of her intelligence when she cries. The public reacts all the more unfavorably to intelligent films that disguise themselves as melo-drama—as in *Le Ciel est à vous* by Jean Grémillon. No film could pre-dispose its audience more unfavorably than *Limelight,* which has all the surface appearance of a great tearjerking melodrama but which con-stantly plays havoc with the viewer's emotions. There is not the slightest trace here of irony or parody which could serve as an intellectual guide-post, a recognizable manner. Chaplin is not trying to deviate from the con-ventions of melodrama as Cocteau did in *Les Parents terribles*—on the contrary, no one has taken himself more seriously. It is simply that situa-tions which start out as conventional are exploited with complete freedom, and without any concern for their traditional meaning. In short, there is nothing in *Limelight* which on the face of it could guarantee it wide public acceptance unless through a misunderstanding. Under these conditions, there nothing reprehensible in the concern of its author to make psycho-logical preparations for its launching; besides, for once the film journalists might justifiably act as accomplices in this.

I will go even further. In my opinion a critical argument of much greater importance can be added to this external justification, itself moral rather than aesthetic. Undoubtedly everyone has the right to have reser-vations about masterpieces—to criticize Racine for Théramène's speech, Molière for his dénouements, Corneille for his awkard handling of the rules. Nor do I suggest there is anything false or barren about such criti-cism. But given a level of artistic creativity, and certainly when faced with evidence of genius, a contrary attitude is necessarily more rewarding. In-stead of thinking of removing so-called faults from a work it is wiser, rather, to be favorably predisposed to them, and to treat them as quali-ties, whose secret we have not so far been able to fathom. This is, I agree, an absurd critical attitude if one has doubts about the object of one's criti-cism; it requires a gamble. One has to "believe" in *Limelight* to become its complete advocate in this way—but there is no lack of reasons for believing in it. The fact that they are not equally evident to everybody simply proves, as Nicole Vedrès says in *Le Cahiers du Cinéma,* that if everyone loved it, it had arrived too late.

However, perhaps I am exaggerating. This defensive criticism will undoubtedly not be valid for every masterpiece, even if one grants that the author is a genius. But it surely does apply to that type of work to which *Limelight* belongs and which I would classify as "meditated" rather than "made" or "thought out." I am speaking of those works which are their own body of reference and whose interior structure might be compared to the stratification of crystals about a central point. Their structure cannot be completely grasped except in relation to this focal point. If one is prepared to see them from the inside, their apparent disorder, their very incoherences, are transformed into a perfect and necessary order. Where it is a question of this kind of artistic creation, it is never the artist who errs but the critic who is slow to grasp the need for a "flaw."

I was confirmed in this view precisely on the evening at the *Comédie Française* when the gods brought together *Don Juan* and Chaplin. How often has one read or heard that Molière's tragicomedy is without doubt his richest work but also his least "well-made"? He wrote it quickly, and its seeming disorder—its chopped-up quality, the breaks in its tone— would all be a natural consequence. To be sure, we are always ready to find a certain charm in these defects, even to forgive them, but never to doubt they are defects. However, it was to the great credit of Jean Meyer's production that it was played at some speed and without an intermission, so that we saw for the first time the perfection of its dramatic structure. It is like some movements in nature that the eye is unable to connect but that the speeded-up camera can reveal to be of a wondrous harmony. Beside *Don Juan, Les Fourberies de Scapin* seems slow and disorganized.

If I may dare to compare them, the resemblances between Molière's masterpiece and *Limelight* go very deep. Like *Don Juan, Limelight* is a work at once deeply pondered and quickly written, revealing beyond doubt Chaplin's most secret heart, borne inside him over a long period, perhaps even unaware, but brought forth in an interval of time that allowed for few changes or second thoughts—while ordinarily Chaplin spent months or even a year on his films. The speed with which it was made, or rather the rapid development of this last and visible stage, instead of producing blemishes and weakness gives the work the impeccable harmony proper to something arising directly from the unconscious. I am not arguing here in favor of romantic inspiration, rather on the contrary for a psychology of creation calling at one and the same time for genius, reflection, and a fine spontaneity in execution. It is precisely these conditions that I find fulfilled in *Limelight*.

That is why I find that a predisposition to admiration for the film is the most prudent critical approach, more rewarding and more certain than one that ifs and buts. Almost everybody praises the second half, but many deplore the *longueurs* and the talkiness of the first half. However, if one were truly responsive to the last 24 minutes of the film, in retrospect one could not imagine a different opening. It becomes apparent that even the boredom one might experience enters mysteriously into the harmony of the over-all work. In any case, what do we mean here by the word boredom? I have seen *Limelight* three times and I admit I was bored three times, not always in the same places. Also, I never wished for any shortening of this period of boredom. It was rather a relaxing of attention that left my mind half free to wander—a daydreaming about the images. There were also many occasions on which the feeling of length left me during the screening. The film, objectively speaking a long one (two hours and twenty minutes), and slow, caused a lot of people, myself included, to lose their sense of time. I see that this phenomenon and the special nature of my periodical boredom have a common cause, namely that the structure of *Limelight* is really more musical than dramatic. I find this confirmed by the English pressbook of the film, three quarters of which is devoted to the music of *Limelight,* to the importance that Chaplin attached to it, and to strange details such as that before he rehearsed a scene, Chaplin would have the score played so as to steep himself in its musical content. In which case time in *Limelight* would be essentially not that of the drama but the more imaginary duration of music, a time that is more demanding on the mind but also leaves it free of the images that nourish it, a time that can be embroidered.

Certainly the principal obstacle to a satisfactory criticism of *Limelight* is the work's fundamental ambiguity. Undoubtedly there is not a single essential ingredient of the scenario of this dubious melodrama, which on analysis is not revealed to be fundamentally ambiguous. Let us look for example at the character of Calvero. Since we tend to think of him in the likeness of Charlie, we do not doubt that we are here dealing with a brilliant clown whose reputation in his great days was not overrated. But nothing could be less certain. Chaplin's real theme is not the decline of the clown through old age and the fickleness of the public, but something more subtle—the value of the artist and the evaluation of his public. Nothing in the film allows us to attribute to Calvero more than a talent for a solid traditional craft. None of his numbers is original—not even the one of the shrinking legs: Grock did it, doubtless following many others. Besides he repeats it twice, leaving us to conclude that his repertoire is not very varied. Are his routines even funny? We are told in the film that they *were* funny, but not that they are so objectively, independent of public approval. And that is the real point. The value of Calvero, his talent and his genius, are not an objective reality affected by varying fortunes, but a fact relative to success itself. As a clown Calvero exists only "for the others." He knows himself only as reflected in the public mirror. Chaplin is not asserting that, inversely, there have never been great artists who were misunderstood and that success or failure are the only true realities of the theater; he is asserting only that the artist is incomplete without his public, that the public does not grant or withhold its approval like an object added to something or subtracted from it, but that this approval consitutes the theatrical personality. We shall never know whether Calvero had genius, and he is less likely to know than we are. What does his glorification by friends who remember him prove? Does not a collective emotion come in here—like the one the audience felt over *Limelight* because Chaplin came to the opening? What is the value of a favorable prejudice such as this? If the audience felt sympathetic, might this not have been as a result of the drinks that were served? Such self-interrogation, lying deep in the heart of the clown as an actor, is at once repudiated and asked for by Calvero. As one grows old, he says, one aspires to be dignified. The actor is less than a man, because he needs other people before he can fulfill himself, because at every appearance he throws himself on their mercy. The wisdom of an aging Calvero is to attain to a serenity beyond success and failure but without denying his art. He knows and affirms that life, just life itself, is the supreme good, but he who is called to be an artist may never renounce his vocation. "I do not love the theater," says Calvero, "neither can I stand the sight of the blood that circulates in my veins."

The theme of theater and of life grasped in all its ambiguity is combined with the Faustian theme of old age. Drink has ruined Calvero but it is old age that prevents him from setting foot, however tentatively, upon the boards again. Just as *Limelight* is not exactly the story of the downfall of a clown, the relation between Calvero and Theresa cannot be reduced to a renunciation of youth by old age. To begin with it is not certain that Theresa does not genuinely love Calvero. It is rather he that persuades her that her feeling for him is unlikely. Of the two it is he who has the freer heart, he who suffers less from their separation; old age is in no sense a weakness, it embodies more strength, more faith in life than does Theresa's youth. Calvero is the anti-Faust, a man who knows how to grow old and renounce Marguerite, who had been captivated by his advanced age. And yet *Limelight* is the most moving of the tragedies of old age, and there can be no questioning this, remembering those wonderful shots in which all the weariness of the world finds its way into this tired mask: the dressing-room scene of the taking off of the make-up, or of the old clown pacing restlessly in the wings during the ballet.

If we compare Calvero now with Chaplin himself as the film compels us to do, the ambiguities of the work are raised to further heights. For, after all, Calvero is at once Chaplin and his opposite. First, and irrefutably, by the identity of the faces. It is not by chance that Chaplin here for the first time is clean-shaven and tells us the story of an aging clown. But, secondly, the truth about Chaplin is the opposite of Calvero's failure: in his art as in his life, Chaplin is a Calvero whose fabulous fame has never known eclipse and who at sixty married a girl of eighteen like Theresa, by whom he has five lovely children. All the same, the Socratic wisdom of Calvero in the midst of his misfortunes may not differ so greatly from that of Mr. Chaplin, showered with success and love. It is difficult not to see Calvero as the shadow thrown by Chaplin—what the most prestigious author of all times might have been if success had abandoned him (as it abandoned Keaton for example) and if Oona, less sure of herself, had believed, like Theresa, that her love was only a profound pity. But at the same time one must admit that in his hour of happiness Chaplin has known how to fashion the wisdom that would have allowed him to put up with Calvero's lot—otherwise, where would Calvero have found it? Still, one must surmise that the possibility makes Chaplin shudder and haunts his nights—else why would he have made *Limelight*?

For *Limelight* can be likened to an exorcising of its author's fate. Calvero is at once Chaplin's fear and his victory over that fear. A double victory, first because the phantom of failure is therein objectivized, incarnated by the person it could haunt, and furthermore because the fallen artist of the film has something better than the strength to recapture his serenity; he is able to justify himself in the success of a young being who will carry his venture forward. When the camera pulls away from Calvero lying dead in the wings and goes to the ballerina onstage, dancing despite her grief, its movement seems to follow transmigration of souls: the theater and life go on.

Here we come to the basic originality of *Limelight*: its " confessional" side, or the "portrait of the author" which shocks some people. Still, such things have long been accepted in literature. I am not talking only about literary "journals" whose explicit purpose this is, but about many novels which are more or less transpositions of the author's life story. Besides, the most impersonal works are not always the least immodest. LoDuca recalls in *Cahiers du Cinéma,* apropos of *Limelight,* the phrase borrowed by Vittorini for the preface to *Conversazione in Sicilia*: "Every work is an autobiography even if the subject is Genghis Kahn, or the New Orleans cemetery." Flaubert says, "Madame Bovary is me." The expression is only astonishing or shocking when it is a question of the cinema, and this can be explained in two ways:

First, its relative novelty, even though the works of von Stroheim for example, or in France of Jean Vigo, are also an endless moral confession. True, the relation is not so explicit, but the more personal nature of Chaplin's confidences constitute a progression, a proof of the maturity of his art. Charlie was a moral silhouette, a marvelous aggregate of symbols; his existence, totally metaphysical, was that of the myth. *Monsieur Verdoux* presupposes already a dialectic relation between the myth and its author —an awareness of Charlie outside the character. Beyond that it only remained for Chaplin to throw away his mask and speak to us face to face, his countenance laid bare. Everyone agrees that when one sees *Limelight* it is impossible to separate what we know of "Charlie," from what we know of Chaplin—but this knowledge does not differ essentially from the tendency of all contemporary criticism of great works, which serves to feed our admiration by way of an ever-deepening knowledge of the lives of their authors. This knowledge of the author's life is not an end in itself, but it allows us to discover new relations which clarify and enrich our understanding of the works. In Chaplin's case the process is simply reversed. The prodigious popularity of its author and of his earlier works put the contemporary spectator in a privileged position that the next generation will not be able to enjoy. Already many young people between fifteen and twenty lack our points of reference and are unable to look back and see Calvero in the light of the Chaplin myth. Is this to say that *Limelight* is valueless except as it relates to Charlie and to Chaplin and that its significance will disappear with time? Certainly not—no more than that works of an autobiographical character demand a deep knowledge of literary history. You do not need a textbook to read Villon's *Ballade des Pendus* or Rousseau's *Confessions*. Many novels and plays *à clef* fade into oblivion because they roused interest solely by reason of indiscretion or curiosity, and this is what distinguishes them from works of real importance in which the author has dealt with his own misery in the perspective of our human condition. If a hundred years from now we came across *Limelight* and no record remained either of Chaplin or his works, that face of his, the deep melancholy of those eyes, would still be enough to tell us that from beyond the grave a man is talking to us about himself, and that he is calling us to witness his life because it too is life, our life. The screen has never before given so clear an example of transposed autobiography, principally because genuine authors are rare in the cinema; the vast majority of directors, even the best of them, are far from possessing the creative freedom enjoyed by the writer. Even when he writes his own screenplay, the film maker remains primarily a director, that is to say a master craftsman who organizes objective elements. Such working conditions are sufficient to warrant artistic creation and the development of style but they lack that total identification, that biological cohesion often found in other arts—between Van Gogh and his painting, between Kafka and his novels. Claude Mauriac has rightly pointed out that Chaplin makes the cinema serve him while others make themselves its servant. In other words, he is the artist in the fullest sense of the term, one who meets art on an equal footing. If he expresses himself by way of cinema, it is not so much because his talents and gifts are more readily adapted to it than for example to literature, but because the cinema can express what he has to say more effectively. The great artists of the late sixteenth century were primarily painters and architects because painting and architecture were the arts of their time. But this was only the best way of being an artist, not of serving a particular art. However, it was thanks to this absence of humility—not toward art but toward the particular forms in which it is categorized today—that the art par excellence of the Renaissance, painting, made such great progress. Leonardo was no more a painter than Michelangelo was a sculptor; they were just artists. That Chaplin, who composes music, has his moments of philosophizing, and even draws a little, is a mediocre musician, a second-rate philosopher, and a Sunday painter, is unimportant. What is crucial is not Chaplin's objective freedom to choose the cinema but the subjective freedom of his relations with the twentieth-century art par excellence, the film. Chaplin is perhaps the only example to date of a creative person who has totally subordinated the cinema to what he had to say, without worrying about conforming to the specifics of its techniques.

Yet this is what some reproach him for—those who have confidence in literature because it passes through the confessional box of language, but who find public confession lacking in modesty. A theatrical art, an hyperbole of incarnation because of the overwhelming physical presence of the image, the cinema is actually the most immodest of the arts. Therefore, by the same token, it calls for the maximum of modesty: for mask and disguise, in style, in subject matter, in make-up. Chaplin in *Limelight* half removes the first two, the third he renounces entirely. *Ecce homo.*

Doubtless nothing short of his genius could have succeeded in such an audacious undertaking, drawing its meaning from the very popularity of the Chaplin myth, and therefore comprehending in its premises the maximum risk of pride and immodesty. In France we have a caricature of this in Sacha Guitry. He had to be sure of public affection to go on about himself, to tens of millions of people, with such seriousness and such conviction: sure of himself too to remove the mask that had made him so loved. But the most admirable thing of all is not that—it is that *Limelight* should be, because of its personal references, so searing, so pure; it is that the trancendence of its message, far from being weighted down by its incarnation, should on the contrary derive from this its most spiritual strength. The greatness of *Limelight* is one with the greatness of the cinema itself— it is the most dazzling display of its very essence, abstraction *by way of* incarnation. Undoubtedly only the unique position of Chaplin, the universality and vitality of his myth (we must not forget that he is still shared today by the Communists and the Western world) allow us to take the dialectic measure of the cinema. Chaplin-Calvero, the twentieth-century Socrates, drinks the hemlock in *public*. But his wisely chosen death cannot be conveyed in words. It is first and foremost in the public exhibition he makes of it, daringly based on the flesh and blood ambiguity of the cinematographic image: see and understand!

It is ridiculous to talk of immodesty here; on the contrary, we should marvel that thanks to the cinema and to Chaplin's genius, the most profound and simple truth may take on a countenance—no longer even that of the actor (and what an actor!) but of a man whom each of us loves and knows, a countenance that speaks to him personally, face to face, in the secret places of the heart, in the darkness.

Chaplin is the only film director whose work stretches over forty years of the history of cinema. The genre in which he first appeared and was triumphant, the silent comedy, was already in its decline before the arrival of sound. Sound finished off Harry Langdon and Buster Keaton, who could not truly survive the genre in which they had shown genius. Von Stroheim's life as a director lasted no more than five years. The average duration of film genius is somewhere between five and fifteen years. Those who hold on longer owe it to intelligence and talent rather than to genius. Only Chaplin has been capable, I will not say of adapting himself to the evolution of the film, but of continuing to be the cinema. Since *Modern Times,* the last of his films to come directly out of the primitive genre of Mack Sennett and the last of his virtually silent films, Chaplin has never stopped moving forward into the unknown, rediscovering the cinema in relation to himself. Alongside *Limelight,* all other films, even those we most admire, seem cut and dried and conventional. Although they may express their author's views, although they may have a personal style, they are only original in part; they conform to some film usages, they are defined by current conventions, even when they contravene them. *Limelight* is like no other film, above all like no other Chaplin film.

It would be an understatement to say that this man of sixty-four is still in the vanguard of the cinema. At one stroke, he has forged ahead of everyone else; more than ever, he remains an example and a symbol of creative freedom in the least free of the arts.

THE WESTERN: OR THE
AMERICAN FILM PAR EXCELLENCE

THE WESTERN is the only genre whose origins are almost identical with those of the cinema itself and which is as alive as ever after almost half a century of uninterrupted success. Even if one disputes the quality of its inspiration and of its style since the thirties, one is amazed at the steady commercial success which is the measure of its health. Doubtless the western has not entirely escaped the evolution of cinema taste—or indeed taste, period. It has been and will again be subjected to influences from the outside—for instance the crime novel, the detective story, or the social problems of the day—and its simplicity and strict form have suffered as a result. We may be entitled to regret this, but not to see in it a state of decay. These influences are only felt in a few productions of relatively high standing and do not affect the low-budget films aimed principally at the home market. Furthermore, it is as important for us to marvel at the western's capacity to resist them as to deplore these passing moments of contamination. Every influence acts on them like a vaccine. The microbe, on contact, loses its deadly virulence. In the course of fifteen years, the American comedy has exhausted its resources. If it survives in an occasional success, it is only to the extent that, in some way, it abandons the rules that before the war made for successful comedy. From *Underworld* (1927) to *Scarface* (1932) the gangster film had already completed the cycle of its growth. The scenarios of detective stories have developed rapidly, and if it is still possible to rediscover an aesthetic of violence within the framework of the criminal adventure which they share with *Scarface,* we would be hard put to see in the private eye, the journalist, or the G-man the reflection of the original hero. Furthermore, if there is such a genre as the American detective film one cannot attribute to it the independent identity of the western; the literature which preceded it has continued to influence it, and the latest interesting variants of the crime film derive directly from it.

On the contrary, the durability of the western heroes and plots has been demonstrated recently by the fabulous success on television of the old Hopalong Cassidy films. The western does not age.

Its world-wide appeal is even more astonishing than its historical survival. What can there possibly be to interest Arabs, Hindus, Latins, Germans, or Anglo-Saxons, among whom the western has had an uninterrupted success, about evocations of the birth of the United States of America, the struggle between Buffalo Bill and the Indians, the laying down of the railroad, or the Civil War!

The western must possess some greater secret than simply the secret of youthfulness. It must be a secret that somehow identifies it with the essence of cinema.

It is easy to say that because the cinema is movement the western is cinema *par excellence.* It is true that galloping horses and fights are its usual ingredients. But in that case the western would simply be one variety of adventure story. Again, the continuous movement of the characters, carried almost to a pitch of frenzy, is inseparable from its geographical setting and one might just as well define the western by its set—the frontier town and its landscapes; but other genres and schools of filmmaking have made use of the dramatic poetry of the landscape, for example the silent Swedish film, but although it contributed to their greatness it did not insure their survival. Better still, sometimes, as in *The Overlanders,* a western theme is borrowed—in this case the traditional cattle drive—and set in a landscape, central Australia, reasonably like the

American West. The result, as we know, was excellent. But fortunately no attempt was made to follow up this paradoxical achievement, whose success was due to an unusual combination of circumstances. If in fact westerns have been shot in France against the landscapes of the Camargue, one can only see in this an additional proof of the popularity and healthiness of a genre that can survive counterfeiting, pastiche, or even parody.

It would be hopeless to try to reduce the essence of the western to one or other of these manifest components. The same ingredients are to be found elsewhere but not the same benefits that appear to go with them. Therefore, the western must be something else again than its form. Galloping horses, fights, strong and brave men in a wildly austere landscape could not add up to a definition of the genre nor encompass its charms.

Those formal attributes by which one normally recognizes the western are simply signs or symbols of its profound reality, namely the myth. The western was born of an encounter between a mythology and a means of expression: the saga of the West existed before the cinema in literary or folklore form, and the multiplication of western films has not killed off western literature which still retains its public, and continues to provide screenwriters with their best material. But there is no common measure between the limited and national audience for western stories and the worldwide audience for the films which they inspire. Just as the miniatures of the *Books of Hours* served as models for the statuary and the stained-glass windows of the cathedrals, this western literature, freed from the bonds of language, finds a distribution on the screen in keeping with its size—almost as if the dimensions of the image had become one with those of the imagination.

This book [J.-L. Rieupeyrout's *La Grande adventure du western 1894-1964,* for which Bazin was here writing the Preface] will emphasize a little-known aspect of the western: its faithfulness to history. This is not generally recognized—primarily, doubtless, because of our ignorance, but still more because of the deeply rooted prejudice according to which the western can only tell extremely puerile stories, fruits of a naïve power of invention that does not concern itself with psychological, historical, or even material verisimilitude. True, few westerns are explicitly concerned with historical accuracy. True, too, these are not the only ones of any value.

It would be absurd to judge the characters of Tom Mix—still more of his magic white horse—or even of William Hart or Douglas Fairbanks, all of whom made lovely films in the great primitive period of the western, by the yardstick of archeology.

After all, many current westerns of honorable standing—I am thinking of *Beyond the Great Divide, Yellow Sky,* or *High Noon*—have only a tenuous relation to historical fact. They are primarily works of imagination. But one would be as much in error not to recognize the historical references in the western as to deny the unabashed freedom of its screenplays J.-L. Rieupeyrout gives a complete account of the birth of its epiclike idealization, based on comparatively recent history, yet it could be that his study, concerned to recall to us what is ordinarily forgotten, or even not known, and confining itself to films that justify his thesis, discards by implication the other side of the aesthetic reality. Still, this would show him to be doubly right. For the relations between the facts of history and the western are not immediate and direct, but dialectic. Tom Mix is the opposite of Abraham Lincoln, but after his own fashion he perpetuates Lincoln's cult and his memory. In its most romantic or most naïve form, the western is the opposite of a historical reconstruction. There is no difference between Hopalong Cassidy and Tarzan except for their costume and the arena in which they demonstrate their prowess. However, if one wanted to take the trouble to compare these delightful but unlikely stories and to superimpose on them, as is done in modern physiognomy, a number of negatives of faces, an ideal western would come through, composed of all the constants common to one and to the other: a western made up solely of unalloyed myth. Let us take one example, that of the woman.

In the first third of the film, the good cowboy meets the pure young woman—the good and strong virgin, let us call her—with whom he falls in love. Despite its chasteness we are able to guess this love is shared. However, virtually insurmountable obstacles stand in its way. One of the most significant and most frequent comes from the family of the beloved—for example, her brother is a sinister scoundrel and the good cowboy is forced to rid society of him, man to man. A modern Chimène, our heroine refuses to see in her brother's assassin any sort of a fine fellow. In order to redeem himself in his charmer's eyes and merit forgiveness, our knight must now pass through a series of fabulous trials. He ends by saving his elected bride from a danger that could be fatal to her person, her virtue, her fortune, or all three at once. Following which, since we are now near the end of the film, the damsel would indeed be ungrateful if she did not feel that her suitor had repaid his debt, and allow him to start dreaming of lots of children.

Up to this point, this outline into which one can weave a thousand variants—for example, by substituting the Civil War for the Indian threat, cattle rustlers—comes close to reminding us of the medieval courtly romances by virtue of the preeminence given to the woman and the trials that the finest of heroes must undergo in order to qualify for her love.

But the story is often complicated by a paradoxical character—the saloon B-girl—who as a rule, is also in love with the cowboy. So there would be one woman too many if the god of the screenwriter was not keeping watch. A few minutes before the end, the prostitute with the heart of gold rescues the man she loves from some danger or another, sacrificing her life and her hopeless love for the happiness of her cowboy. This also serves to redeem her in the eyes of the spectators.

There is food for thought here. Note, first of all, that the distinction between good and bad applies only to the men. Women, all up and down the social scale, are in every case worthy of love or at least of esteem or pity. The least little prostitute is redeemed by love and death—although she is spared the latter in *Stagecoach* with its resemblance to de Maupassant's *Boule de Suif*. It is true that the good cowboy is more or less a reformed offender so that henceforth the most moral of marriages with his heroine becomes possible.

Furthermore, in the world of the western, it is the women who are good and the men who are bad, so bad that the best of them must redeem themselves from the original sin of their sex by undergoing various trials. In the Garden of Eden, Eve led Adam into temptation. Paradoxically Anglo-Saxon puritanism, under the pressure of historical circumstances, reverses the Biblical situation. The downfall of the woman only comes about as a result of the concupiscence of men.

Clearly, this theory derives from the actual sociological conditions obtaining in primitive western society which, because of the scarcity of women and the perils of a too harsh existence in this burgeoning world, make it imperative to safeguard its female members and its horses. Hanging was considered enough punishment for stealing a horse. To engender respect for women more was needed than the fear of a risk as trifling as the loss of one's life, namely the positive power of a myth. The myth of the western illustrates, and both initiates and confirms woman in her role as vestal of the social virtues, of which this chaotic world is so greatly in need. Within her is concealed the physical future, and, by way of the institution of the family to which she aspires as the root is drawn to the earth, its moral foundation.

These myths, of which we have just examined what is perhaps the most significant example (the next is the myth of the horse) may themselves doubtless be reduced to an even more essential principle. Basically each of these particularize, by way of an already specific dramatic plot, the great epic Manicheism which sets the forces of evil over against the knights of the true cause. These immense stretches of prairie, of deserts, of rocks to which the little wooden town clings precariously (a primitive amoeba of a civilization), are exposed to all manner of possible things. The Indian, who lived in this world, was incapable of imposing on it man's order. He mastered it only by identifying himself with its pagan savagery. The white Christian on the contrary is truly the conqueror of a new world. The grass sprouts where his horse has passed. He imposes simultaneously his moral and his technical order, the one linked to the other and the former guaranteeing the latter. The physical safety of the stagecoaches, the protection given by the federal troops, the building of the great railroads are less important perhaps than the establishment of justice and respect for the law. The relations between morality and law, which in our ancient civilization are just a subject for an undergraduate paper, were half a century ago the most vital thing confronting the youthful United States. Only strong, rough, and courageous men could tame these virgin lands. Everyone knows that familiarity with death does not keep alive the fear of hell, nor do scruples or moral debate. Policemen and judges are of most help to the weak. It was the force of this conquering humanity that constituted its weakness. Where individual morality is precarious it is only law that can impose the order of the good and the good of order.

But the law is unjust to the extent that it pretends to guarantee a moral society but ignores the individual merits of those who constitute that society. If it is to be effective, this justice must be dispensed by men who are just as strong and just as daring as the criminals. These virtues, as we have said, are in no way compatible with virtue in the absolute sense. The sheriff is not always a better person than the man he hangs. This begets and establishes an inevitable and necessary contradiction. There is often little moral difference between the outlaw and the man who operates within the law. Still, the sheriff's star must be seen as constituting a sacrament of justice, whose worth does not depend on the worthiness of the man who administers it. To this first contradiction a second must be added, the administration of justice which, if it is to be effective, must be drastic and speedy—short of lynching, however—and thus must ignore extenuating circumstances, such as alibis that would take too long to verify. In protecting society, such a form of justice runs the risk of unkindness to the most turbulent though not perhaps the least useful nor even the least deserving of its children.

Although the need for law was never more clearly allied to the need for morality, at the same time never was their antagonism more concrete and more evident. It is this which provides a basis, within a slapstick framework, for Charlie's *Pilgrim,* at the conclusion of which we see our hero riding his horse along the borderline between good and evil, which also happens to be the Mexican border.

John Ford's *Stagecoach,* which is a fine dramatic illusration of the parable of the pharisee and the publican, demonstrates that a prostitute can be more respectable than the narrow-minded people who drove her out of town and just as respectable as an officer's wife; that a dissolute gambler knows how to die with all the dignity of an aristocrat; that an alcoholic doctor can practice his profession with competence and devotion; that an outlaw who is being sought for the payment of past and possibly future debts can show loyalty, generosity, courage, and refinement, whereas a banker of considerable standing and reputation runs off with the cashbox.

So we find at the source of the western the ethics of the epic and even of tragedy. The western is in the epic category because of the superhuman level of its heroes and the legendary magnitude of their feats of valor. Billy the Kid is as invulnerable as Achilles and his revolver is infallible. The cowboy is a knight-at-arms. The style of the *mise en scène* is in keeping with the character of the hero. A transformation into an epic is evident in the set-ups of the shots, with their predilection for vast horizons, all-encompassing shots that constantly bring to mind the conflict between man and nature. The western has virtually no use for the closeup, even for the medium shot, preferring by contrast the traveling shot and the pan which refuse to be limited by the frameline and which restore to space its fullness.

True enough. But this epic style derives its real meaning only from the morality which underlies and justifies it. It is the morality of a world in which social good and evil, in their simplicity and necessity, exist like two primary and basic elements. But good in its natal state engenders law in all its primitive rigor; epic becomes tragedy, on the appearance of the first conflict between the transcendence of social justice and the individual character of moral justice, between the categorical imperative of the law which guarantees the order of the future city, and the no less unshakeable order of the individual conscience.

The Corneille-like simplicity of western scripts has often been a subject for parody. It is easy to see the analogy between them and the text of *Le Cid*: there is the same conflict between love and duty, the same knightly ordeals on the completion of which the wise virgin will consent to forget the insult to her family; the same chaste sentiments which are based on a concept of love subordinated to respect for the laws of society and morality. But this comparison is double-edged: to make fun of the western by comparing it to Corneille is also to draw attention to its greatness, a greatness near perhaps to the child-like, just as childhood is near to poetry.

Let there be no doubt about it. This naïve greatness is recognized in westerns by simple men in every clime—together with the children—despite differences of language, landscape, customs, and dress. The epic and tragic hero is a universal character. The Civil War is part of nineteenth century history, the western has turned it into the Trojan War of the most modern of epics. The migration to the West is our Odyssey.

Not only is the historicity of the western not at odds with the no less evident penchant of the genre for outlandish situations, exaggerations of fact and the use of the *deus ex machina* (in short, everything that makes for improbability); it is, on the contrary, the foundation of its aesthetic and its psychology. The history of film has only known one other epic cinema and that too is a historical cinema. Our purpose here is not to compare epic form in the Russian and in the American film, and yet an analysis of their styles would shed an unexpected light on the historical meaning of the events reconstructed in the two of them. Our only purpose is to point out that it is not their closeness to the facts that has given them their styles. There are legends that come into being almost instantaneously, that half a generation suffices to ripen into an epic. Like the conquest of the West, the Soviet revolution is a collection of historical events which signal the birth of a new order and a new civilization. Both have begotten the myths necessary for the confirmation of history, both had to reinvent a morality to rediscover at their living source and before mixture or pollution took place, the foundation of the law which would make order out of chaos, separate heaven from earth. But perhaps the cinema was the only language capable of expressing this, above all of giving it its true aesthetic dimension. Without the cinema the conquest of the West would have left behind, in the shape of the western story, only a minor literature, and it is neither by its painting nor its novels that Soviet art has given the world a picture of its grandeur. The fact is that henceforth the cinema is the specifically epic art.

THE EVOLUTION OF THE WESTERN

BY THE EVE of the war the western had reached a definitive stage of perfection. The year 1940 marks a point beyond which some new development seemed inevitable, a development that the four years of war delayed, then modified, though without controlling it. *Stagecoach* (1939) is the ideal example of the maturity of a style brought to classic perfection. John Ford struck the ideal balance between social myth, historical reconstruction, psychological truth, and the traditional theme of the western *mise en scène*. None of these elements dominated any other. *Stagecoach* is like a wheel, so perfectly made that it remains in equilibrium on its axis in any position. Let us list some names and titles for 1939-1940: King Vidor: *Northwest Passage* (1940), Michael Curtiz: *The Santa Fe Trail* (1940), *Virginia City* (1940); Fritz Lang: *The Return of Frank James* (1940), *Western Union,* (1940); John Ford: *Drums Along the Mohawk* (1939); William Wyler: *The Westerner* (1940)· George Marshall, *Destry Rides Again,* with Marlene Dietrich, (1939).*

This list is significant. It shows that the established directors, having perhaps begun their careers twenty years before with serial westerns made almost anonymously, turn (or return) to the western at the peak of their careers—even Wyler whose gift seemed to be for anything but this genre.

---

* A disappointing remake of this film was shot in 1955 by the same George Marshall, with Audie Murphy.

This phenomenon can be explained by the widespread publicity given westerns between 1937 and 1940. Perhaps the sense of national awareness which preceded the war in the Roosevelt era contributed to this. We are disposed to think so, insofar as the western is rooted in the history of the American nation which it exalts directly or indirectly.

In any case, this period supports J.-L. Rieupeyrout's argument for the historical realism of the western.*

But by a paradox more apparent than real, the war years, properly so-called, almost removed the western from Hollywood's repertoire. On reflection this is not surprising. For the same reason that the westerns were multiplied and admired at the expense of other adventure films, the war film was to exclude them, at least provisionally, from the market.

As soon as the war seemed virtually won and even before peace was definitely established, the western reappeared and was again made in large numbers, but this new phase of its history deserves a closer look.

The perfection, or the classic stage, which the genre had reached implied that it had to justify its survival by introducing new elements. I do not pretend to explain everything by the famous law of successive aesthetic periods but there is no rule against bringing it into play here. Take the new films of John Ford. *My Darling Clementine* (1946) and *Fort Apache* (1948) could well be examples of baroque embellishment of the classicism of *Stagecoach*. All the same, although this concept of the baroque may account for a certain technical formalism, or for the relative preciousness of this or that scenario, I do not feel that it can justify any further complex evolution. This evolution must be explained doubtless in relation to the level of perfection reached in 1940 but also in terms of the events of 1941 to 1945.

Let us call the ensemble of forms adopted by the postwar western the "superwestern." For the purposes of our exposé this word will bring together phenomena that are not always comparable. It can certainly be justified on negative grounds, in contrast to the classicism of the forties and to the tradition of which it is the outcome. The superwestern is a

---

* *Le Western ou le cinéma américain par excellence,* Collection Septième Art, Editions du Cerf, Paris, 1953.

western that would be ashamed to be just itself, and looks for some additional interest to justify its existence—an aesthetic, sociological, moral, psychological, political, or erotic interest, in short some quality extrinsic to the genre and which is supposed to enrich it. We will come back later to these adjectives. But first we should indicate the influence of the war on the evolution of the western after 1944. The phenomenon of the superwestern would probably have emerged anyway, but its content would have been different. The real influence of the war made itself deeply felt when it was over. The major films inspired by it come, naturally, after 1945. But the world conflict not only provided Hollywood with spectacular scenes, it also provided and, indeed, forced upon it, some subjects to reflect upon, at least for a few years. History, which was formally only the material of the western, will often become its subject: this is particularly true of *Fort Apache* in which we see the beginning of political rehabilitation of the Indian, which was followed up by numerous westerns up to *Bronco Apache* and exemplified particularly in *Broken Arrow* by Delmer Daves (1950). But the profounder influence of the war is undoubtedly more indirect and one must look to find it wherever the film substitutes a a social or moral theme for the traditional one. The origin of this goes back to 1943 with William Wellman's *Oxbow Incident,* of which *High Noon* is the distant relation. (However, in Zinnemann's film it is also a rampant McCarthyism that is under scrutiny.)

Eroticism also may be seen to be at least an indirect consequence of the war, so far as it derives from the triumph of the pin-up girl. This is true perhaps of Howard Hughes' *The Outlaw* (1943). Love is to all intents and purposes foreign to the western. (*Shane* will rightly exploit this conflict.) And eroticism all the more so, its appearance as a dramatic springboard implying that henceforth the genre is just being used as a foil the better to set off the sex appeal of the heroine. There is no doubt about what is intended in *Duel in the Sun* (King Vidor, 1946) whose spectacular luxury provides a further reason, albeit on formal grounds, to classify it as a superwestern.

Yet *High Noon* and *Shane* remain the two films that best illustrate the mutation in the western genre as an effect of the awareness it has gained

151

of itself and its limits. In the former, Fred Zinnemann combines the effect of moral drama with the aestheticism of his framing. I am not one of those who turn up their noses at *High Noon*. I consider it a fine film and prefer it to Stevens' film. But the great skill exemplified in Foreman's adaptation was his ability to combine a story that might well have been developed in another genre with a traditional western theme. In other words, he treated the western as a form in need of a content. As for *Shane* this is the ultimate in "superwesternization." In fact, with it, George Stevens set out to justify the western—by the western. The others do their ingenious best to extract explicit themes from implied myths but the theme of *Shane* is the myth. In it Stevens combines two or three basic western themes, the chief being the knight errant in search of his grail, and so that no one will miss the point, Stevens dresses him in white. White clothes and a white horse are taken for granted in the Manichean world of the western, but it is clear that the costume of Alan Ladd carries with it all the weighty significance of a symbol, while on Tom Mix it was simply the uniform of goodness and daring. So we have come full circle. The earth is round. The superwestern has gone so far beyond itself as to find itself back in the Rocky Mountains.

If the western was about to disappear, the superwestern would be the perfect expression of its decadence, of its final collapse. But the western is definitely made of quite other stuff than the American comedy or the crime film. Its ups and downs do not affect its existence very much. Its roots continue to spread under the Hollywood humus and one is amazed to see green and robust suckers spring up in the midst of the seductive but sterile hybrids that some would replace them by.

To begin with, the appearance of the superwestern has only affected the more out-of-the-ordinary productions: those of the A-film and of the superproduction. These surface tremors have not disturbed the commercial nucleus, the central block of the ultracommercial westerns, horseback or musical, which may even have found a second youth on television. (The success of Hopalong Cassidy is a witness to this and proves likewise the vitality of the myth even in its most elementary form.) Their acceptance by the new generation guarantees them several more cycles of years to come. But low-budget westerns never came to France and we have to be satisfied with an assurance of their survival from the personnel of American distribution companies. If their aesthetic interest, individually, is limited, their existence on the other hand is probably decisive for the general health of the genre. It is in these "lower" layers whose economic fertility has not diminished that the traditional western has continued to take root. Superwestern or no superwestern, we are never without the B-western that does not attempt to find refuge in intellectual or aesthetic alibis. Indeed, maybe the notion of the B-film is open to dispute since everything depends on how far up the scale you put the letter A. The productions I am talking about are frankly commercial, probably fairly costly, relying for their acceptance only on the reputation of their leading man and a solid story without any intellectual ambitions. *The Gunfighter,* directed by Henry King (1950) and starring Gregory Peck, is a splendid example of this attractive type of production, in which the classic theme of the killer, sick of being on the run and yet forced to kill again, is handled within a dramatic framework with great restraint. We might mention too *Across the Wide Missouri,* directed by William Wellman (1951), starring Clarke Gable, and particularly *Westward the Women* (1951) by the same director.

In *Rio Grande* (1951), John Ford himself has clearly returned to the semiserial format, or at any rate to the commercial tradition—romance and all. So it is no surprise to find on this list an elderly survivor from the pioneer days of old, Allan Dwan, who for his part has never forsaken the old Triangle* style, even when the liquidation of McCarthyism gave him the chance to broaden the scope of the old-time themes (*Silver Lode,* 1954).

I have still a few more points to make. The classification I have followed up to now will turn out to be inadequate and I must no longer explain the evolution of the western genre by the western genre itself. Instead I must take the authors into greater account as a determining factor. It will doubtless have been observed that the list of relatively traditional pro-

---

* An amalgamation of three American film-production companies, Keystone, KayBee, and Fine Arts.

ductions that have been little influenced by the superwestern includes only names of established directors who even before the war specialized in fast-moving adventure films. It should come as no surprise that their work affirms the durability of the western and its laws. Howard Hawks, indeed, at the height of the vogue of the superwestern should be credited with having demonstrated that it had always been possible to turn out a genuine western based on the old dramatic and spectacle themes, without distracting our attention with some social thesis, or, what would amount to the same thing, by the form given the production. *Red River* (1948) and *The Big Sky* (1952) are western masterpieces but there is nothing baroque or decadent about them. The understanding and awareness of the means matches perfectly the sincerity of the story.

The same goes for Raoul Walsh, all due allowances being made, whose film *Saskatchewan* (1954) is a classical example of a borrowing from American history. But his other films provide me—and I am sorry if it is a little contrived—with the transition I was looking for: *Colorado Territory* (1949), *Pursued* (1947) and *Along the Great Divide* (1951) are, in a sense, perfect examples of westerns just above the B-level, made in a pleasantly traditional dramatic vein. Certainly there is no trace of a thesis. We are interested in the characters because of what happens to them and nothing happens that is not in perfect accord with the western theme. But there is something about them that, if we had no information about their date, would make us place them at once among more recent productions, and it is this "something" that I would like to define.

I have hesitated a great deal over what adjective best applies to these westerns of the fifties. At first I thought I ought to turn to words like "feeling," "sensibility," "lyricism." In any case I think that these words must not be dismissed and that they describe pretty well the character of the modern western as compared with the superwestern, which is almost always intellectual at least to the degree that it requires the spectator to reflect before he can admire. All the titles I am about to list belong to films that are, if not less intelligent than *High Noon* at least without *arrière-pensée,* and in which talent is always a servant of history and not of the meaning behind history. There is another word, maybe more suitable than those I have suggested or which provides a useful complement—the word "sincerity." I mean by this that the directors play fair with the genre even when they are conscious of "making a western." At the stage to which we have come in the history of the cinema naïveté is hardly conceivable, but although the superwestern replaces naïveté by preciousness or cynicism, we have proof that it is still possible to be sincere. Nicholas Ray, shooting *Johnny Guitar* (1954) to the undying fame of Joan Crawford, obviously knows what he is about. He is no less aware of the rhetoric of the genre than the George Stevens of *Shane,* and furthermore the script and the director are not without their humor; but not once does Ray adopt a condescending or paternalist attitude toward his film. He may have fun with it but he is not making fun of it. He does not feel restricted in what he has to say by the limits of the western even if what he has to say is decidedly more personal and more subtle than its unchanging mythology.

It is with an eye on the style of the narrative, rather than on the subjective attitude of the director to the genre, that I will finally choose my epithet. I say freely of the westerns I have yet to name—the best in my view—that they are "novelistic." By this I mean that without departing from the traditional themes they enrich them from within by the originality of their characters, their psychological flavor, an engaging individuality, which is what we expect from the hero of a novel. Clearly when one talks about the psychological richness of *Stagecoach,* one is talking about the way it is used and not about any particular character. For the latter we remain within the established casting categories of the western: the banker, the narrow-minded woman, the prostitute with a heart of gold, the elegant gambler, and so on. In *Run for Cover* (1955) it is something else again. The situation and characters are still just variations on the tradition, but what attracts our interest is thir uniqueness rather than their generosity. We know also that Nicholas Ray always treats his pet subject, namely the violence and mystery of adolescence. The best example of this "novelization" of the western from within is provided by Edward Dmytryk in *Broken Lance* (1954), which we know is only a western remake of Mankewicz's *House of Strangers.* For the uninformed, *Broken Lance* is simply a western that is subtler than the others with more individualized characters and more complex relationships but which stays no less rigidly within the limits of two or three classic themes. In point of fact, Elia Kazan has treated a psychologically somewhat similar subject with great simplicity in his *Sea of Grass (1947),* also with Spencer Tracy. We can imagine many intermediate grades between the most dutiful B-western and the novelistic western, and my classification is inevitably arbitrary.

Nevertheless I offer the following idea. Just as Walsh is the most remarkable of the traditional veterans, Anthony Mann could be considered the most classical of the young novelistic directors. We owe the most beautifully true western of recent years to him. Indeed, the author of *The Naked Spur* is probably the one postwar American director who seems to have specialized in a field into which others have made only sporadic incursions. In any case, each of Mann's films reveals a touching frankness of attitude toward the western, an effortless sincerity to get inside its themes and there bring to life appealing characters and to invent captivating situations. Anyone who wants to know what a real western is, and the qualities it presupposes in a director, has to have seen *Devil's Doorway* (1950) with Robert Taylor, *Bend of the River* (1952) and *The Far Country* (1954) with James Stewart. Even if he does not know these three films, he simply has to know the finest of all, *The Naked Spur* (1953). Let us hope that CinemaScope will not rob Anthony Mann of his natural gift for direct and discreet use of the lyrical and above all his infallible sureness of touch in bringing together man and nature, that feeling of the open air, which in his films seems to be the very soul of the western and as a result of which he has recaptured—but at the level of the hero of the novel and no longer of the hero of the myth—the great lost secret of the Triangle days.

The above examples show that a new style and a new generation have come into existence simultaneously. It would be both going too far and naïve to pretend that the novelistic western is just something created by young men who came to film-making after the war. You could rightly refute this by pointing out that this quality is evident in *The Westerner,* for example, and there is something of it in *Red River* and *The Big Sky.* People assure me, although I am personally not aware of it, that there is much of it in Fritz Lang's *Rancho Notorious* (1952). At all events it is certain that King Vidor's excellent *Man Without a Star* (1954) is to be placed in the same perspective, somewhere between Nicholas Ray and Anthony Mann. But we can certainly find three or four films made by the veterans to place alongside those that the younger men have made. In spite of everything, it is chiefly the newcomers who delight in the western that is both classic and novelistic: Robert Aldrich is the most recent and brilliant example of this with his *Apache* (1954) and expecially his *Vera Cruz* (1954).

There remains now the problem of CinemaScope. This process was used for *Broken Lance, Garden of Evil* (1954) by Henry Hathaway (a good script at once classic and novelistic but treated without great inventiveness), and *The Kentuckian* (1955) with Burt Lancaster which bored the Venice Festival to tears. I only know one film in CinemaScope that added anything of importance to the *mise en scène,* namely Otto Preminger's *River of No Return* (1954), photographed by Joseph LaShelle. Yet how often have we not read or have even ourselves written that while enlarging of the screen is not called for elsewhere, the new format will renew the westerns whose wide-open spaces and hard riding call out for wide horizons. This deduction is too pat and likely sounding to be true. The most convincing examples of the use of CinemaScope have been in psychological films such as *East of Eden.* I would not go so far as to say that paradoxically the wide screen is unsuitable for westerns or that it adds nothing to them, but it seems to me already an accepted fact that CinemaScope will add nothing decisive to this field.*

The western, whether in its standard proportions, in Vistavision, or on a super-wide screen, will remain the western we hope our grandchildren will still be allowed to know.

---

* We have a reassuring example of this in *The Man from Laramie* (1955), in which Anthony Mann does not use CinemaScope as a new format but as an extension of the space around man.

ENTOMOLOGY OF THE PIN-UP GIRL

FIRST, LET US not confuse the pin-up girl with the pornographic or erotic imagery that dates from the dark backward and abysm of time. The pin-up girl is a specific erotic phenomenon, both as to form and function.

Definition and Morphology

A wartime product created for the benefit of the American soldiers swarming to a long exile at the four corners of the world, the pin-up girl soon became an industrial product, subject to well-fixed norms and as stable in quality as peanut butter or chewing gum. Rapidly perfected, like the jeep, among those things specifically stipulated for modern American military sociology, she is a perfectly harmonized product of given racial, geographic, social, and religious influences.

Physically, this American Venus is a tall, vigorous girl whose long, streamlined body splendidly represents a tall race. Different from the Greek ideal, with its shorter legs and torso, she thus differs distinctly from European Venuses. With her narrow hips, the pin-up girl does not evoke motherhood. Instead, let us note particularly the firm opulence of her bosom. American eroticism—and hence cinematic eroticism—seems to have moved in recent years from the leg to the breast.

The parading of Marlene Dietrich and of her legs, with their almost mathematically perfect contours, the success of Rita Hayworth, the success (this time *de scandale*) in Howard Hughes' film *The Outlaw* of Jane Russell, whose twin hemispheres were inflated by an airborne publicity campaign to the size of clouds, are an indication of this sweeping displacement in the geography of sex appeal—or rather, since the term is already out of date, in "man appeal." The vanguard of feminine attractiveness stands today at the level of the heart. I offer as proof reports which reach us from Hollywood, and the suit that Paulette Goddard has brought against a journalist who dared to suggest that she wore falsies.

An adequate physique, a young and vigorous body, provokingly firm breasts still do not define the pin-up girl for us. She must also conceal that bosom, which we are not supposed to get a peep at. The clever kind of censorship which clothing can exercise is perhaps more essential than the most unmistakable anatomic affirmation.

The typical garment of the pin-up girl is the two-piece bathing suit—which coincides with the limitations authorized socially by fashion and modesty in recent years. At the same time, however, an infinite variety of suggestive degrees of undress—never exceeding some rigorously defined limits—show off to advantage the charms of the pin-up girl while pretending to hide them. For my part, I am inclined to consider these niceties somewhat decadent: a contamination of the pure pin-up with traditional erotic imagery. At any rate, it is only too obvious that the veils in which the pin-up girl is draped serve a dual purpose: they comply with the social censorship of a Protestant country which otherwise would not have allowed the pin-up girl to develop on an industrial and quasi-official scale; but at the same time make it possible to experiment with the censoring itself and use it as an additional form of sexual stimulus. The precise balance between the requirements of censorship and the maximum benefits one can derive from them without lapsing into an indecency too provocative for public opinion defines the existence of the pin-up girl, and clearly distinguishes her from the salaciously erotic or pornographic postcard.

The science of these forms of provocative undress has been developed to a nicety: today Rita Hayworth need only take off her gloves to draw admiring whistles from a hall full of Americans.

Metamorphosis of the Pin-up Girl

The multiplication and absurdity of today's supporting decors in contrast to the childlike and unsophisticated simplicity of the first pin-ups, can be explained by the need felt by the artist or photographer to vary his presentation. There are several thousand ways to show a pretty girl in a bathing suit, but certainly not hundreds of thousands. But as we see it, this development is a disintegration of the ideal of the pin-up girl.

A wartime product, a weapon of war, with the coming of peace the pin-up has lost her essential *raison d'être*. In the process of its revival this wartime myth is being separated into its two components, eroticism and morality. On the one hand, the pin-up girl tends to revert to the category of sex imagery and all its hypocritical vestiary complications; on the other to post-mobilization domestic virtues. Furthermore, in the United States there are even contests for "pin-up mothers" and "pin-up babies." And finally, the advertisers of tonic waters, chewing gum, and cigarettes are trying to convert the various salvageable surpluses for peacetime purposes.

Philosophy of the Pin-up Girl

In a general history of eroticism, and more specifically in a history of eroticism as it relates to the cinema, the pin-up girl embodies the sexual ideal of the future. In *Brave New World* Aldous Huxley tells us that when children are produced in test-tubes, relations between men and women, sterile henceforth, will have no other purpose than unrestricted pleasure. Huxley neatly sums up the ideal of beauty and female sexual attractiveness in an epithet that is at once tactile, muscular, and visual, the adjective "pneumatic." Is not the pneumatic girl of Huxley the archetype, projected into the future, of the Varga girl? In a long-drawn-out, distant war of invasion, the feminine ideal necessarily represents imagination, sterility, play. The pin-up girl is the expression of this ideal, extended to the pure status and scope of a myth, in a society where Protestantism still maintains a vigilant censorship.

The Pin-up and the Cinema

If I have had little to say of cinema up to this point, it is because the pin-up girl is not originally part of it. The pin-up was not born on the screen but on magazine covers, on the fold-outs of *Esquire,* on the cut-out pages of *Yank.* Subsequently the cinema adopted this erotic mythology as its own, and soon the American star resembled the drawings of Varga.

The screen already had a solid tradition in this field. The women in clinging bathing suits who people the trick-shot skies of Georges Méliès derived, too, from a naïvely erotic imagery whose glory, at the turn of the century, was the princess of Caraman-Chimay. A little later, in America, Mack Sennett, that astute precursor in the field foresaw clearly the popularity of the bathing suit, but the performances of his bathing beauties as a group, rather like those of the music hall, gave no hint as yet of the higly individual future of the pin-up girl and the star. Thus the cinema from its beginning was predisposed to the use of the pin-up, and reciprocally to reinforce the feminine ideal she represents in the imagination and taste of the public.

I do not value this kind of cinematic eroticism very highly. Produced by special historical circumstances, the feminine ideal reflected in the pin-up girl is in the last analysis (despite its apparent anatomical vigor) extremely artificial, ambiguous, and shallow. Sprung from the accidental sociological situation of the war, it is nothing more than chewing gum for the imagination. Manufactured on the assembly line, standardized by Varga, sterilized by censorship, the pin-up girl certainly represents a qualitative regression in cinematic eroticism. Lillian Gish in *Broken Blossoms,*

161

Dietrich in *The Blue Angel,* Garbo, now Ingrid Bergman—are after all quite different from Rita Hayworth!

In 1931 the stars were living on grapefruit and hiding their bosoms. At the same time, the tidal wave of the Hays office censorship was breaking over Hollwood. The danger, though seeming to come from the opposite direction, was at bottom the same: phoniness. Cinematic eroticism wasted away in artifice and hypocrisy. Then came Mae West. The Mae West of the future will doubtless not have the generous curves of a Fifi Peachskin. But neither will she have to react against the same artificialities and shams; shocking or chaste, shy or provocative, all the American cinema needs from her is more authenticity.

THE OUTLAW

"The best of women is not worth a good horse."

EVEN BEFORE it was shown in France, *The Outlaw* had acquired a scandalous reputation that was bound to result in public disappointment and make it a subject of severe criticism. In the event, the film had a short run. The same people who had fought to get to see it during the first days of its run booed those sections from which they thought the most interesting scenes had been cut. They felt robbed. Reviewers for the most part adopted an indulgent and amused tone. It would have been undignified to show disappointment. One critic managed to see something else in it besides the absence of Jane Russell's breasts. After all, he knew beforehand what he was dealing with: it would have been naïve to expect more from the Americans. But even the more aggressive critics did not make out a particularly convincing case for seeing in the film yet another example of Hollywood's decline and standardization. To argue against the hypocrisy of American moralizing was too easy. And too easy also to extol the good old French bosoms of Rabelais' nuns, or Molière's servant girls, or even the amorous stories of the eighteenth century, as opposed to this canned eroticism, as deceptive and flavorless as those California fruits which are insipid even to the worms. Surely, no one saw here the sinister hand of the Marshall Plan intending to replace the real bosoms of Jacqueline Pierreux or Dany Robin by the deceptive pneumaticism of a Jane Russell. Undeniably, *The Outlaw* foundered in a sea of general indifference.

I am inclined to see in this limited attention paid to the Howard Hughes film first an injustice and second a tacit conspiracy of silence. The careless way in which the film was dismissed in no more than a line or two, the unmistakable absence of any passionate feeling, seemed to me more assumed than genuine. I am afraid the assets of Jane Russell have been treated like the sour grapes in the fable. If not, then how do we explain that one of the most erotic films ever made and one of the most sensational scripts ever filmed by Hollywood has been so little noticed?

The Outlaw is a western. It preserves the framework and the majority of the traditional themes of a western and some of the characteristic types of the genre—particularly the lovable and devious sheriff whom we were so delighted to meet in Wyler's *The Westerner*. In a film that has retained such a purity of form as the western any originality is measured by the slight changes that have been made to the traditional ingredients, the skill with which the screenwriter and director have succeeded in simultaneously remaining faithful to the basic rules of the genre and still renewing our delight. Jules Furthman, Howard Hughes, and Gregg Toland have concentrated their efforts on the style and on an unexpected switch in the female element, which in the Far West has generally been represented by two types of heroine, reflecting two complementary aspects of the same myth[1]. The prostitute with the heart of gold in *Stagecoach* is on a par in the spectator's judgment with the courageous virgin, rescued by the good cowboy from extreme danger, whom he will marry once he has proved himself and triumphed over evil. Frequently he takes the place in the girl's life of her father or her brother killed in a fight. Thus we see clearly drawn in the western not only the obvious quest for the Holy Grail but in a more precise sociological and aesthetic degree the mythology of chivalry founded on the essential goodness of woman, even the sinful woman. It is man who is bad. Isn't he indeed the cause of her downfall, in spite of which the prostitute manages to preserve something of her original purity? It is the hero's role to redeem the evil in man by undergoing trials, in order to win back the respect and the protection that woman demands of him.

It is this mythology that Howard Hughes attacks, with a violence that I have found nowhere in the American cinema except in *Monseur Verdoux*.

The Outlaw is based on contempt for woman. In contrast to their conterparts elsewhere, its heroes strive to deny the heroine their protection. They scoff at her endlessly, abandon her, and refuse to undergo any trials. In this unbelievable anti-quest of the Holy Grail it is the woman who needs them and who undergoes the severest tests before her master will bestow a kind glance on her. From beginning to end Jack Beutel and Walter Huston share Jane Russell, and these two sympathetic and courageous men, capable of killing one another over a horse, absolutely refuse to fight over her.

It is clear that Howard Hughes has knowingly given a general significance to his heroine. Jane Russell is not a woman who particularly deserves such treatment. The absence of any other female character who might save the good name of her sex, reminding us that "they are not all like that" through some comparison unfavorable to the heroine, is also significant. After all, Jane Russell is not at all antipathetic. A woman of courage, she has sworn to revenge her brother, and it is only after having conscientiously tried to kill her lover, first with a revolver and then with a pitchfork, that she is raped by him. Chimène, after all, did no better. One cannot reproach her for renouncing her vengeance after making love. She will henceforth love with as much fervor and fidelity as she has once sought vengeance. The man will even owe her his life on the night when, ill and shivering and at his last gasp from a deathly chill, Jane Russell presses her naked body against his.*

To tell the truth, this woman is no worse than any other. There is nothing about her to give a moral justification for the men's cynicism and contempt for her. In the logic of the film Jane Russell does not deserve any particular treatment; these men simply think women are always treated better than they deserve.

It is no accident that the real scenario is the story of three jealous males. Two of them, Billy the Kid (Jack Beutel) and Doc Holliday (Walter

---

* Reminiscent of *The River* by Frank Borzage. The crow is replaced here by a starving rooster that gobbles up eyes.

Huston) sleep with the same woman—but they love the same horse. On several occasions they come near to killing one another over the horse, but in the end they retain their friendship. This provokes the jealousy of Thomas Mitchell, who thinks he is Huston's only friend. So it is that these men are incapable of jealousy except over a horse or over each other. They constitute a Spartan group in which women have no emotional role. Women are only to sleep with or to do the cooking.

It is understandable in such circumstances that the film was banned by the American censors for four years. The official complaint was the daring of some scenes, but the real objection, which was more or less admitted, was to the basic idea of the script. It is forbidden to despise women. Even the misogyny apparent in the American crime film some years earlier is a far cry from the cynicism of *The Outlaw*. The blonde murderess of these films is presented as a kind of female criminal; even the men are bad. In *The Outlaw* no one is antipathetic; it is the order of the universe that confers his preeminence on man and makes a domestic animal out of woman—pleasant but boring, not as interesting as an animal.

Still, *The Outlaw* should not disappoint a perceptive viewer, even on the level at which the censors tried to deal with it. I remarked earlier that those who were disappointed by the film are either insincere or lacking in perception. Admittedly one does not "see" very much. Objectively, if one sticks purely to what is offered to view, *The Outlaw* is quite the most prudish of American films. But it is precisely upon the spectator's frustration that its eroticism is built. Suppose for a moment that the film had been made in some European country. The Swedes and Danes would have given us a front and side view of the heroine naked; the French would have plunged the neckline of her dress to the navel and treated the spectator to some sensational kissing scenes, the Germans would have shown us just the breasts, but all of them; the Italians would have put Jane Russell into a little black nightgown and there would have been some sizzling love scenes. Altogether it it is Hollywood alone that is capable of making such a film without showing us a thing. Yet whether in a Swedish, French, or Italian version, *The Outlaw* would have much less effect on the viewer's imagination. If an erotic film is one that is capable of provoking the audience to desire the heroine sexually and of keeping that desire alive, the technique of provocation is here brought to the peak of perfection, to the point where we see nothing but the shadow of a breast.

I strongly suspect Howard Hughes and Gregg Toland of having played an outrageous trick on the censor. It is surely not an accident that the director of *The Outlaw* was an associate of the director of *Sullivan's Travels*. Preston Sturges and Howard Hughes were made to understand one another. These two men knew how to structure their work on what for others would be a limitation. Preston Sturges understood that the mythology of the American comedy had arrived simultaneously both at saturation point and the point of exhaustion. There was no way to make use of it other than to take its excesses as the subject of a scenario. Furthman and Hughes had fun here by forcing the censors into pornography. On reflection, the real director of *The Outlaw* was not Howard Hughes. It was Mr. Hays. If he had been as free as a novelist to use his medium, the director would not have been forced to proceed by way of hints, to suggest rape by noises in the dark and a woman's body by the edge of a low-necked dress. In such a case the film would certainly have been improved aesthetically, but we would have been deprived of a delightful satire on censorship. Tartuffe's handkerchief is placed on this bosom in so obvious a way that not even a three-year-old child could resist the temptation to pull it off. From unsatisfied desire to obsession . . .

And so it is that Mr. Hays caters to the erotic dreams of millions of citizens—all good fathers, good husbands, good fiancés. What leads me to believe that the makers of the film knew exactly what they were doing, is the staggering skill with which they were able to play on the fine edges of the censorship code and not overstep the authorized limits by a hair's breadth, while constantly making us conscious of the moral prohibition that weighed on their undertaking. Otherwise *The Outlaw* would have been just a daring film, violent and realistic. It was the censorship code that turned it into an erotic film. Gregg Toland must have had great fun lighting the throat of Jane Russell, scrupulously focusing on that milk-white patch barely hollowed by a shadow, whose mere presence had the frustrated spectators dithering with resentment. The critics can perhaps be excused for not having understood *The Outlaw*. All they saw in the film, for the best of reasons, was what they did not see.

For those particularly interested in the phenomenology of Hollywood eroticism, I would like to draw attention to a curious shift of emphasis between the publicity for the film and the film itself. The posters for *The Outlaw* show Jane Russell with lifted skirt and generously low-cut dress. In reality it is only her bosom that counts in the film. The fact is that in the past seven or eight years the center of eroticism in the American film has shifted from the thigh to the bosom, but the public is not yet sufficiently aware of this change of frontier to allow the publicity departments to dispense with their traditional sources of stimulation.

MARGINAL NOTES ON
EROTICISM IN THE CINEMA

NO ONE would dream of writing a book on eroticism in the theater. Not, strictly speaking, because the subject does not lend itself to reflection, but because these reflections would all be negative. Certainly this is not true of the novel, since one whole section of literature is founded, more or less explicitly, on eroticism. But it is only a sector of it, and the existence in the Bibliothèque Nationale of a section known as "hell" points up the fact. It is true that eroticism now tends to play an increasingly important role in modern literature, and novels are full of it, even the popular ones. But aside from the fact that one should doubtless attribute this spread of eroticism largely to the cinema, eroticism remains subject to moral notions of a more general nature which compel us to treat the spreading of it as a problem. Malraux, who among contemporary novelists has assuredly most lucidly expounded an ethic of love based on eroticism, illustrates equally perfectly the modern, historic, and thus relative nature of such a choice. In short, eroticism tends to play a role in contemporary literature similar to that of courtly love in medieval literature. But no matter how powerful its myth, and no matter what future we may foresee for it, eroticism has clearly no specific connection with the literature of the novel in which it appears. Even painting, in which the representation of the human body might well have played a determining role, is only accidentally or secondarily erotic. Licentious drawings, engravings, prints, or paintings constitute only a genre, a variant coming under the same heading as bawdy writing. One could make a study of the nude in the plastic arts but, though one doubtless could not overlook the transmission thereby of erotic feelings, these still remain a subordinate and secondary phenomenon.

It is of the cinema alone that we can say that eroticism is there on purpose and is a basic ingredient. Not the sole ingredient, of course, for there are many films and good ones that owe it nothing, but a major, a specific, and even perhaps an essential one.

Lo Duca* is right, then, to see one of the constants of cinema in this phenomenon: "For half a century the sheet covering the movie screen has borne like a watermark one basic motto: eroticism." But it is important to know if the ubiquitousness of eroticism, however general, is only an accidental result of the free capitalist play of supply and demand. Needing to attract customers, the procedure would naturally have turned to the most effective stimulus: sex. One might advance in support of this argument the fact that the Soviet cinema is indeed the least erotic in the world. The example deserves thinking about, certainly, but it does not seem conclusive, for one would first have to examine the various cultural, ethnic, religious, and sociological factors which may have come to play in this particular case—and above all one would have to ask whether the puritanism of Soviet films is not a much more artificial and temporary phenomenon than the competition in eroticism among the capitalists. From this point of view the film *The Forty-First* opens up a lot of new horizons.

Lo Duca seems to see the source of cinematic eroticism in the relationship between seeing a movie and dreaming. "The cinema resembles the dream, with its colorless images like those of a film, and this in part explains the lesser erotic intensity of color films, which in a sense escape the rules of the word of dreams."

I will not quarrel with my friend except over details. Where do we get this rooted prejudice that no one ever dreams in color? It cannot be said that

---

* Lo Duca, *Erotisme au cinéma*, Jean-Jacques Pauvert, 1956.

I am the only one who enjoys this privilege. Besides, I have asked around among friends. The fact is, there are dreams in black and white and dreams in color, exactly as in the cinema, depending on the process. The most I will grant Lo Duca is that the production of color films has outstripped that of dreams in Technicolor. But I certainly will not go along with him in his incomprehensible devaluation of eroticism in color. Well, let us attribute these differences to little personal perversions and not spend more time on them. The essential is still the basically dreamlike quality of cinema, of the moving image.

If this hypothesis is correct, the psychology of the viewer would tend to be identical with that of the sleeper dreaming. And we know that in the last analysis all dreams are erotic.

But we also know that the censorship which presides over dreams is infinitely more strict than all the Mrs. Grundies of the world. The superego of each of us is, unbeknownst, a Mr. Hays. Hence the extraordinary repertory of symbols, general and specific, whose job it is to disguise from our conscious minds the impossible scenarios of our dreams.

Consequently the analogy between dreams and cinema should be extended even further. It lies no less in what we deeply desire to see on the screen than in what could never be shown there. It is a mistake to equate the word "dream" with some anarchic freedom of the imagination. In fact nothing is more predetermined and censored than dreams. It is true, and the surrealists do well to remind us, that this is not due to our reason. It is true also that it is only in a negative sense that censorship can be said to determine the dream, and that its positive reality, on the contrary, lies in the irresistible transgression of the superego's prohibitions. I am aware too of the difference between cinematographic censorship, which is social and legal, and dream censorship; I only want to point out that the function of censorship is essential to cinema and dreams alike. It is a dialectical constituent of them.

It is this which seems to me to be lacking in Lo Duca's preliminary analysis, and still more in his enormous collection of illustrations, which constitute a documentation that falls doubly short. The author *does* know, of course, how exciting things can be that the censor formally prohibits,

171

but he sees them only as a last resort; above all, the intelligence directing the choice of his illustrations exemplifies the contrary thesis. It would have been better to show us what the censor habitually cuts out of films, rather than what he lets pass. I am not denying the interest and certainly not the charm of what the censor leaves in, but I do think, in the case of Marilyn Monroe, that the obligatory photo was not the one from the calendar in which she posed nude (especially since this extra-cinematographic document antedated her success as a star and so cannot be considered a further extension of her sex appeal on the screen) but rather the famous scene from *The Seven-Year Itch* in which the air from the subway grating blows up her skirt. This inspired idea could only be born in the world of a cinema with a long, rich, byzantine tradition of censorship. Inventiveness such as this presupposes an extraordinary refinement of the imagination, acquired in the struggle against the rigorous stupidity of a puritan code. Hollywood, in spite and because of the taboos that dominate it, remains the world capital of cinematic eroticism.

I am not saying, however, that all true eroticism has to outwit an official code of censorship before it can blossom on the screen. In fact, what is gained by such surreptitious transgression can be more than offset by what is lost. The social and moral taboos of the censors are too arbitrary and stupid to be able to channel the imagination suitably. Though helpful in comedy or film-ballet, for example, they are just a hindrance, dumb and insurmountable, in realistic films.

Thus the one critical censorship that the cinema cannot dispense with is imposed by the image itself, and in the last analysis it is in relation to the image and the image alone that we must attempt to define the psychology and the aesthetics of erotic censorship. I certainly do not intend to outline it here even in the broadest terms, but rather to propose a series of ideas which, linked up, may indicate a direction in which one might explore further.

Before anything else, I must give credit for whatever merit these remarks may have to Jean Domarchi, for they stem from a comment he made to me which seems extraordinarily pertinent and fruitful.

Domarchi, then, who is no prude, told me that he has always been irritated at the orgy scenes on the screen, or in somewhat more general terms, by any erotic scene incompatible with the impassiveness of the actors. In other words, it seemed to him that erotic scenes had to be able to be played like any others, and that actual sexual emotion by the performers in front of the camera was contradictory to the exigencies of art. This austere view at first seems surprising, but it is founded on an irrefutable argument, and on one not resting on moral grounds. If you can show me on the screen a man and woman whose dress and position are such that at least the beginnings of sexual consummation undoubtedly accompanied the action, then I would have the right to demand, in a crime film, that you really kill the victim—or at least wound him pretty badly. Nor is this hypothesis ridiculous, for it is not too long ago that killing stopped being a spectacle. The executions in the Place de Grève were just that, and for the Romans the mortal combat in the circus were the equivalents of orgies. I once wrote, apropos of a notorious newsreel sequence showing officers of Chiang Kai-shek's army executing "Communist spies" in the streets of Shanghai, that the obscenity of the image was of the same order as that of a pornographic film. An ontological pornography. Here death is the negative equivalent of sexual pleasure, which is sometimes called, not without reason, "the little death."

The theater would never tolerate anything like this. On the stage everything that relates to the physical side of love derives from the paradox of the actor. No one is ever aroused sexually at the Palais-Royal—neither on the stage nor in the audience. Strip tease, it is true, poses another question, but we can agree that strip tease has nothing to do with the theater, even if it is a spectacle and observe further that it is essential that the woman herself does the undressing. She could not be undressed by a partner without provoking the jealousy of the entire male audience. In reality, the strip tease is based on the polarization and stimulation of desire in the spectators, each one potentially possessing the woman who pretends to offer herself—but if anyone were to leap on the stage he would be lynched, because his desire would then be competing with, and in opposition to, that of all others (unless it turned into an orgy and "voyeurism," which involve a different mental mechanism).

173

In the cinema, on the other hand, even a nude woman can be approached by a partner, openly desired, and actually caressed; because unlike the theater, an actual acting space based on consciousness and conflict, the cinema unreels in an imaginary space which demands participation and identification. The actor winning the woman gratifies me by proxy. His seductiveness, his good looks, his daring do not compete with my desires—they fulfill them.

But if the cinema held to this psychology alone, it would idealize pornographic films. On the contrary, it is clear that if we wish to remain on the level of art, we must stay in the realm of imagination. I ought to be able to look upon what takes place on the screen as a simple story, an evocation which never touches the level of reality, at least unless I am to be made an accomplice after the fact of an action or at least of an emotion which demands secrecy for its realization.

This means that the cinema can say everything, but not show everything. There are no sex situations—moral or immoral, shocking or banal, normal or pathological—whose expression is *a priori* prohibited on the screen, but only on condition that one resorts to the capacity for abstraction in the language of cinema, so that the image never takes on a documentary quality.

This is why *And God Created Woman* seems to me, despite some good qualities that I recognize, in part a detestable film.

I have put forward my argument, developing logically the remark made by Domarchi. I have now to admit my embarrassment in face of the objections that arise. They are numerous. To begin with, I cannot hide from myself the fact that I have brushed off a good part of the contemporary Swedish cinema. It will be noticed, however, that the masterpieces of eroticism seldom succumb to this criticism. Stroheim himself seems to me to escape it. Sternberg too.

But what troubles me most about the fine logic of my argument is a sense of its limitations. Why do we stop with the actors and not bring the onlooker into the argument? If the aesthetic metamorphosis is perfect, he should be no less impassive than the performers. Rodin's "Kiss," despite its realism, provokes no libidinous thoughts.

Above all, is not the distinction between the literary image and the cinematic image false? To consider the latter as of a different essence because it is achieved photographically implies many aesthetic consequences which I will not discuss. If Domarchi's postulate is correct, it is applicable with proper adaptation to the novel. Domarchi ought to be embarrassed every time a novelist describes acts which he could not imagine with a perfectly cool head. Does the situation of the writer differ all that much from the director and his actors? Only, in these matters the separation of the imagination and the act is fairly dubious, if not arbitrary. To grant the novel the privilege of evoking everything, and yet to deny the cinema, which is so similar, the right of showing everything, is a critical contradiction which I note without resolving.

THE DESTINY OF JEAN GABIN

THE FILM star is not just an actor, not even an actor particularly beloved of the public, but a hero of legend or tragedy, embodying a destiny with which scenarists and directors must comply—albeit unwittingly. Otherwise the spell between the actor and his public will be broken. The variety of films in which he appears, and which seem so agreeably surprising in their novelty, should not mislead us. It is the confirmation of a destiny, profound and essential, which we unconsciously seek in the actor's continually renewed exploits. This is evident in Chaplin, for example, and, interestingly enough, more secretly and subtly illustrated in a star like Jean Gabin.

In nearly all Gabin films—at least from *La Bête humaine* to *Au-delà des grilles*—he comes to a violent end that has the appearance, more or less, of suicide. Is it not strange that the commercial law of the happy ending, which forces so many producers to tack on artificial finales like those of the Molière comedies, is not valid for one of the most popular and sympathetic actors—whom everyone should wish to see happily married with lots of children?

But can you see Gabin as a family man? Could anyone imagine that, at the end of *Quai des Brumes,* he had managed to snatch poor Michèle Morgan from the clutches of Michel Simon and Pierre Brasseur, and sailed with her to a future in America; or that, having come to his senses, he preferred when day broke in *Le Jour se lève* to turn himself in and hope for a probable acquittal?

No, it is impossible. The public that swallows many affronts would undoubtedly feel that they were being taken for a ride if screenwriters presented them with a happy ending for Jean Gabin.

Proof by a *reductio ad absurdum*: let someone try to kill off Luis Mariano or Tino Rossi in the same fashion!

How can we explain this paradox, all the more glaring because it contradicts an inviolable law of the cinema? The explanation is that Gabin, in the films referred to, is not just giving an interpretation of one story among many others. It is always the same story—his own, and one which must inevitably end unhappily, like the story of Oedipus or Phaedra. Gabin is the tragic hero of the contemporary cinema. With every new Gabin film the cinema rewinds the infernal machine of his destiny—just as in *Le Jour se lève,* that night, as on every night, he winds up the alarm clock whose ironic and cruel ringing will sound at daybreak the hour of his death.

It would be a simple matter to show how, under cover of an ingenious diversity, the essential gears of the mechanism remain identically the same. Here is one example. Before the war, it is said, Gabin insisted before signing any film contract that the story include one of those explosive scenes of anger at which he excels. Was this the whim of a star, was it the ham clinging to his little touch of bravura? Perhaps, but he probably felt, through his actor's vanity, that to deprive himself of it would betray his character. Indeed it is almost always in a moment of rage that Gabin brings misfortune on himself, baiting the fateful trap that will inevitably cause his death. Besides, in the tragedies and epics of ancient times anger was not just a psychological state amenable to treatment by a cold shower or a sedative; it was a special state, a divine possession, an opening for the gods into the world of humanity, through which destiny steals. Thus in a gesture of rage Oedipus on the road to Thebes brought misfortune upon himself by killing a charioteer (his father) whom he did not recognize. The modern gods who reign over suburban Thebes with their Olympus of factories and their steel monsters wait too for Gabin at the crossroads of fate.

What I have said holds good more for the prewar Gabin of *La Bête humaine* and *Le Jour se lève*. Gabin has changed since then; he is older, his formerly blond hair is gray, his face has grown fatter. In the cinema, we used to say, destiny does not take on a countenance, it is the countenance that reveals its destiny. Gabin could not remain the same forever; but neither could he escape from a mythology that is so solidly established.

And thus, significantly, Aurenche and Bost in *Au-delà des grilles* have taken over where Jeanson and Prevért left off. We remember the last shot of *Pépé le Moko*: the dying Gabin clinging to the iron railings around Algiers harbor, watching the ship that carries all his hopes sail away. René Clément's film begins where Duvivier's ended. Its titles might save said, "Suppose Gabin had been given a chance—he could have caught the boat; here he is now, on the other side of the railings." The film is simply Gabin's return to his fate, the quasi-voluntary renunciation of love and happiness, the admission that a paroxysm of toothache and the gods, when all is said and done, are the strongest forces in life.

Admittedly in *La Marie du Port* the force of destiny is softened. Gabin becomes merely an actor again. For the first time, he gets married—but will he be any happier? Marcel Carné has not been able to escape paying his dues to the old myth. Gabin is rich, he is a "success"—nevertheless, throughout the film there is talk of a ship in dry dock, or a trawler that never sets sail, and is there like a witness to the old dream Gabin never achieved (the dream of an escape he could never make, a parting that would set him free). Thus his present dubious happiness, his material rather than moral success, is nothing more than a confession of failure, the paltry reward of an act of renunciation. The gods are merciful to those who no longer seek to be heroes.

It remains for the sociologists and moralists (specifically the Christian moralists—and why not the theologians?) to reflect on the profound meaning of a mythology in which, through the popularity of an actor like Gabin, millions of our contemporaries rediscover themselves. Perhaps a world without God becomes a world of the gods and of the fates they dispense.

SOURCES AND TRANSLATOR'S NOTES

AN AESTHETIC OF REALITY: NEOREALISM
(CINEMATIC REALISM AND THE ITALIAN SCHOOL OF THE
LIBERATION)
From *Esprit,* January, 1948

P. 17, Centro Sperimentale di Cinematografia.
This school was founded in 1935 under Mussolini. The Institut des
Hautes Etudes Cinématographiques was founded in Paris in 1943.

P. 21, Beaumarchais (1732–1799).
Author of *The Barber of Seville* and *Figaro,* the latter revealing Beau-
marchais' capacity for witty and satirical criticism of French society
during the last days of the *ancien régime.* On the eve of World War II
Jean Renoir consciously and successfully paralleled Beaumarchais in
La Règle du jeu.

P. 22, Anna Magnani.
Originally a popular singer in Rome's Trastevere, the equivalent of
Montmartre in Paris or of Cockney London.

P. 26, expressionist heresy.
Heresy because it does not reflect reality as cinema should. It is curious

that Eisenstein and Bazin are in agreement in condemning expressionism (see *Film Form*, p. 203) although their ideas of cinematic realism are not at all the same. (Eisenstein said, "I am not a realist, I am a materialist.")

P. 26, the art of cinema lives off this contradiction. Bazin is implying here what he states more explicitly elsewhere, notably in "The Myth of Total Cinema" *(What Is Cinema?* Vol. I, p. 17.) Cinema tends with each new invention towards a greater realism, the complete achievement of which would mean its own destruction.

P. 28, parallelepiped.
A six-sided prism whose faces are parallelograms. Presumably Bazin wishes here to give a concrete metaphor for his conception of film space as a very real entity with boundaries that can be rigidly visualized.

P. 31, the law of gravity that governs the ordering of the facts. This notion of gravity also appears in the essay on *Cabiria*. Again Bazin uses an analogy from science in distinguishing between the deliberate aesthetic ordering of events and the order that seems to be set up in the sheer weight of the facts themselves, so that they would seem to "tumble vertically into place." This idea of Bazin's strikingly resembles one expressed by the English poet Gerard Manley Hopkins: "Chance left free to act falls into an order as well as purpose."

LA TERRA TREMA
From *Esprit,* December, 1948

P. 41, the exoticism intrinsic to the subject matter. The word "exoticism" is used generally to describe a certain kind of literature and film dealing with places and peoples unfamiliar to the reader or viewer. Bazin describes this type of film in *What Is Cinema?* Vol.

I, p. 155, citing Ruttmann's *Melodie der Welt*. Thus the word has a wider meaning than the one usually attached to it.

P. 43, Bazin's use of technical terms.
French technical film terms are sometimes misleading because they do not always mean what at first sight (or first translation) they appear to mean. A definition of three terms that appear frequently in Bazin's essays may help the reader to avoid the pitfall of literal translation:

Découpage does not mean cutting or editing, though it can bear on this process; it normally means the definitive form or structure of the film as described on paper, as it is to appear later on the screen; its usual English equivalent is "shooting script." *Mise en scène* is a term taken from the theater, meaning the actual creating or structuring of the film by the *metteur en scène* or director. It can be used in a matter-of-fact way, and perhaps should be; but in recent years it has also been given a larger meaning, referring to many elements of a director's style. *Montage* is not necessarily used in the sense in which we commonly employ it, to refer especially to Russian or "classical" montage. In French it frequently refers to the "mounting" or assembling of shots—what we usually call editing or cutting.

P. 46, *Piscator*.
Bazin is referring to the film *The Revolt of the Fishermen,* directed in 1934 at Mezhrapom by the German theater producer Erwin Piscator, founder during World War I of the Proletarian Theater, and in exile in the USSR at the time. Brecht, in his younger days, worked with Piscator and was considerably influenced by him.

BICYCLE THIEF
From *Esprit,* November, 1949

P. 49, populist.
Populism is the name given to a literary school that aimed at a realistic

portrayal of the lives of "the common people." See also Bazin's essay on *Umberto D.*

P. 52, phenomenological integrity.

The event as it appears in itself to the senses and the mind, either before any discourse or, as here, presenting it without dramatic manipulation that may "cheat on reality." See also Bazin's essay on De Sica.

P. 57, limpidity.

Limpidity is a quality both of objects (such as water) and, by analogy, of style. Bazin is here saying that what would normally derive from the style is here derived from the object, or in this case from the event.

P. 58, Roger Leenhardt.

Born 1902. Director and film critic. He was Bazin's film mentor and his predecessor on film subjects in the section of *Esprit* entitled "Journal à plusieurs voix."

P. 58, madeleine.

A light cake; important as a memory stimulant in Proust's *A la recherche du temps perdu.*

P. 59, congenitally a hybrid.

For a discussion of this subject and Bazin's rejection of "pure cinema," see *What Is Cinema?* Vol. I, pp. 53 ff.

P. 60, integral of reality.

As distinct from a reality divided up by montage or distorted by expressionist techniques.

DE SICA, METTEUR EN SCÈNE

This text was originally published in Italian in 1951 by Edizione Guanda, Parma. The English version is based on the French translation.

P. 64, The faithful reproduction of reality is not art.
From this it follows that neither is it cinema, in spite of the reproductive quality of the camera. This aspect of the question *"Is film an art?"* was early treated by Rudolf Arnheim (*Film as Art,* pp. 8 ff.)

P. 64, Naturalism.
Originally a literary movement. Flaubert is considered the founder, followed by the Goncourts, Daudet, Zola, Maupassant, and Huysmans. They wrote novels and plays *à thèse,* applying to the arts the methods and findings of science.

P. 66, Neorealism is an ontological position . . .
because it is concerned with things as they are and events in their phenomenological integrity. Its aesthetic has been dealt with in the previous essay.

P. 66, American neorealism.
Although the movement is not called neorealism in the United States, Bazin is referring presumably to the realism of the writings of W. D. Howells, Dreiser, Hemingway, Faulkner, Dos Passos, and others. The term is sometimes used to describe the work of some Italian post-World War II novelists, notably Pavese and Vittorini. "The term" says Heiney in *America in Modern Italian Literature* (p. 78) "comes from the cinema," and is not very satisfactory outside the cinema.

P. 66, Zavattini is the only one who shamelessly admits to the title.
In this context (and by way of supporting Bazin's arguments) it is interesting to refer to a statement by Zavattini himself. He is speaking of the preparations of a film that was never made, *Italia Mia.* It was to be an experiment in *"a kind of film which had respect for the circumstances in which we live.* It would not merely be the product of the author's imagination which is always to some extent isolated from reality. I hoped that the things-in-themselves could become a story because only in that way it seemed to me could a film-writer really listen to the *cry of reality."*

P. 68, dramatic contingency.

As distinct from the "irreversible fatality" of classic tragedy, with its *necessity* which is the opposite of *"contingent."*

P. 69, loving things in their singular individuality.

Here we have an echo of the epistemology of *Duns Scotus,* Franciscan. The implications of this statement may be deduced from various passages in these essays, most notably those concerning Rossellini and Francis of Assisi, whose love of things is expressed so clearly in his "Canticle of All Created Things." It is an attitude characteristic of a poet and is admirably illustrated in a passage from the Introduction by Robert Bridges to the poems of Gerard Manly Hopkins (Penguin Poets, pp. xxiii, xxiv). "Unlike St. Thomas Aquinas, Scotus attached great importance to individuality and personality. Again where Aquinas had said that the individual is really unknowable (only the universal being known) Scotus declared that the individual on the contrary is immediately knowable by the intellect in union with the senses. By a first act of knowlege, the mind has a correct but vague intuition of the individual concrete object as a most special thing. We can imagine how so much emphasis on the *value of the concrete thing,* the object of sense, must have appealed to the poet in Hopkins." It also helps us to see Scotus as a proto-phenomenologist.

P. 70, the tenderness of De Sica.

In this paragraph the word *ambiguity* once more appears. As we have pointed out in the Introduction Bazin and Amedée Ayfre attach great importance to this "ambiguity of reality." Hence, Bazin here holds himself aloof from both the Christian Democrat and the Communist view and interestingly parallels Christian charity and Marxist class consciousness. One cannot help wondering if his tongue is not in his cheek when he asks: "What party indeed could afford to leave love to the other?" In this same section he refers to love scaling walls and penetrating strongholds. This is one of

184

his many allusions to medieval French literature. Here he is thinking of *Le Roman de la Rose.*

P. 72, Andre Suarès.
Born 1866. A solitary and pessimistically inclined person, haughty and aristocratic. Interested in all forms, in life and art, that exhibit heroism and force. Wrote, among other books, stories of Tolstoy, Pascal, Ibsen and Dostoievsky. *"Le Coeur ignoble de Charlot"* appeared in *Comœdia,* Paris, July 3, 1926. In his reply next day in the same paper, J. Baroncelli said that the attack "revolted and saddened" him.

P. 74, Who steals an egg, steals a bull.
The English equivalent is "He who will steal a pin will steal a pound."

P. 76, A cinema of "duration."
Bazin appears to have in mind here the Bergsonian use of the word *"duration";* Bergson's philosophy was particularly concerned with "time." This is not the only place where Bazin has recourse to Bergsonian terms and concepts (see note on *Cabiria*). Bergson contrasts objective time, "which serves as the framework for concrete reality and subjective time, lived-through time, *duration."* He separates human life "from concrete reality and practical activity" and reduces it "to the experiencing of duration, to the continual flux of states of consciousness." This also explains Bazin's use of the word "psychologism" in the essay on *Cabiria.*

UMBERTO D: A GREAT WORK
From *France-Observateur,* October, 1952

P. 79, Micheline Vian, *Temps Modernes,* January, 1952. This issue contains two articles under the general heading "Points of View about *Miracolo a Milano."* The first, "The Pink and the Black" is by René Guyonnet. The second is "Toto or the Misfortune of Being an

Object." Either Bazin or the printer has in part mistaken the name of the writer, Michelle-L'Eglise Vian. The article is a brilliant and witty analysis of the various opinions expressed by the critics and makes great fun of various shades of party-line interpretations by them. Bazin clearly took in good part the references to him. Vian quotes him as saying in *L'Observateur* that De Sica has solved to his own satisfaction the contradiction between social message and art without betraying art. Bazin himself, she says in this critique, seems to have solved to *his* own satisfaction the problem of "running with the hare and hunting with the hounds" without betraying the interests of either.

P. 79, battle of *Umberto D.*
Bazin is here alluding to the famous episode known as the "battle of *Hernani*," a play by Victor Hugo put on at the Comédie Française, February 25, 1830. A number of distinguished literary figures and members of the general public demonstrated violently against the play as representing the new romantic trend in theater. However, the play survived and triumphed.

CABIRIA: THE VOYAGE TO THE END OF NEOREALISM
From *Cahiers du Cinéma,* November, 1957

P. 84, an effect of vertical gravity. See note on page 76, above.

P. 85, *Données immédiates de la conscience.*
This was the title of Bergson's doctoral thesis written in 1888, subsequently translated into English as *Time and Free Will.*

IN DEFENSE OF ROSSELLINI
From *Cinema Nuovo,* August, 1955

P. 97, naturalism and verism.
See A. Ayfre, "Neorealism et Phenomenologie," *Cahiers du Cinéma,*

No. 17, p. 52. This article also appears in Ayfre's *Conversion aux images* (Editions du Cerf).

P. 98, St. Januarius.
Early Christian martyr. His body was brought to Naples where his blood is kept in a glass phial. On certain days of the year the blood is said to liquefy—an occasion for a Neapolitan celebration.

THE MYTH OF MONSIEUR VERDOUX
From *Revue du Cinéma,* January, 1948

P. 102, *Monsieur Verdoux* was boycotted by the American Legion in the United States, received little exhibition, and was withdrawn; it was a commercial failure in Europe.

P. 102, Sire de Gambais.
Squire of Gambais, which is situated in the Seine-et-Oise and boasts a beautiful seventeenth-century castle—for which it is less generally known than for the murders committed there by the bluebeard Landru.

P. 104, *Princesse de Clèves*.
A novel by Madame de la Fayette (1634–1693), considered the forerunner of the psychological novel.

P. 107, How can you measure his existence by time?
It is interesting to compare this notion with a somewhat similar statement by G. K. Chesterton in his study of Dickens who, he says, did not strictly make a literature, rather he made a mythology. He did not always manage to make his characters men, but he always managed to make them gods. "They are creatures like Punch and Father Christmas. They live statically in a perpetual summer of being themselves."

P. 109, The road of hope.
A phrase taken from a film of the same name, reviewed by Bazin in *Cahiers du Cinéma* (February, 1952). It deals with the hopes of a group of unemployed Sicilian miners who set out for France to look for jobs which have been falsely promised to them.

P. 117, crystallization.
A word adopted into French from Stendhal's *De l'amour*. It refers both to feelings and ideas. The lover delights in embroidering on the perfections of the woman he loves, and complacently reflects upon his happiness. If you put a branch down one of the abandoned mines in Salzburg, after a while it becomes crystallized—covered with a profusion of glittering crystals so that the original branch is unrecognizable. Stendhal wrote that he used the word to describe that operation of the spirit that deduces new perfections from awareness of the old.

P. 117, The thirteenth woman.
This perhaps says the same thing as Cesare Pavese's remark about love: "There is never a first time. The first time is always the second time."

P. 122, planes of cleavage.
Bazin is referring to the quality of some rocks that break more readily in some directions than in others. Homothetic=similar and similarly placed, as any two plane sections of a cone.

LIMELIGHT, OR THE DEATH OF MOLIERE
From *L'Observateur,* November, 1952

P. 126, the lost fame and old age of a man who resembles him like a brother.
For a development of this, see "Chaplin, est-il le frère de Charlot?" by Barthelemy Amengual, *Travail et Culture,* Algiers, 1952. The

phrase is also reminiscent of the refrain of the poem *La Nuit de décembre* by de Musset.

P. 127, buried by torchlight.
Molière (1622-1673) was taken ill on the stage of the old Palais Royal theater and was carried to the rooms of a friend where he died. Actors were forbidden burial in consecrated ground in those days, but in Molière's case royal intervention by Louis XIV overrode ecclesiastical opposition. He was buried at night in a cemetery on the rue Montmartre, but no indication was left of his burial place.

THE GRANDEUR OF *LIMELIGHT*
From Esprit, April, 1953

P. 130, Théramène.
Bazin is referring to the very lengthy speech of Théramène, tutor of Hippolytus, in the fifth act of *Phèdre*.

P. 131, Nicole Vedrès.
This article appeared in *Cahiers du Cinéma,* December, 1952 with a number of others including one by Lo Duca referred to later in this essay, in praise of *Limelight*.

P. 131, *Don Juan*.
In *Cahiers,* December, 1952, Jean Renoir describes the joy of Chaplin at the Comédie Française as he listened to *Don Juan*. "This delight was not feigned. [Chaplin] was at home, and it is always a pleasure to be with one's own kind."

P. 135, Elio Vittorini.
Born in Sicily 1908. Italian novelist and, after Cesare Pavese, the most important of the *Americanisti* of the thirties. Like Pavese, he translated various American novels into Italian, among them *Tortilla Flat*.

THE WESTERN: OR THE AMERICAN FILM PAR EXCELLENCE

Preface to J.-L. Rieupeyrout's *Le Western ou le cinéma américain par excellence,* Editions du Cerf, Paris, 1953.

P. 142, books of hours.

A form of prayer book, originating in the Middle Ages, giving the hymns, psalms, and prayers to be recited at certain times of the day. Some, made for the rich and noble, were beautifully illustrated, notably that of the Duc de Berry.

P. 143, Chimène. See note for *The Outlaw.*

THE ENTOMOLOGY OF THE PIN-UP GIRL

From *Ecran Français,* December 17, 1946.

P. 161, Princesse de Caraman-Chimay.

The princess, from a Belgian family, was an individualist who shocked society at the turn of the century by claiming her right to do anything she liked, including posing in the nude. This was at a time when appearing before an audience in a tight-fitting bathing costume was considered the height of nudity.

THE OUTLAW

From *Revue du Cinéma,* August, 1948.

P. 164, the quest for the Holy Grail.

Some have also seen resemblances between the western and Greek tragedy. This is one of several occasions on which Bazin draws a parallel between the western and courtly romances (see also "Eroticism in the Cinema").

p. 165, Chimène.

Chimène, the heroine of Corneille's *Le Cid,* was in love with a young soldier, who kills her father. Despite her continuing love, she demands the soldier's death.

EROTICISM IN THE CINEMA
From *Cahiers du Cinéma,* April, 1957.

P. 169, Eroticism and courtly love.
The reference here is to the fact that the relationship of courtly love had of necessity to be adulterous. In order to be "worshipped" the lady had to be above her lover in rank. Usually, the object of the knight's devotion was the wife of his feudal lord, as with Arthur, Guinevere, and Lancelot, or in the *Châtelaine de Vergy.*

P. 170, Lo Duca [Joseph-Marie].
Born Milan 1910. Author, journalist, and director of shorts, among them one about Louis Lumière (1949). He was an original member of the editorial board of *Cahiers,* from which he withdrew in 1957.

P. 171, Mrs. Grundy.
The French term Bazin uses is "Anastasie"—a name given to the censorship by artists and writers. She is usually depicted as an ugly old woman armed with an enormous pair of scissors.

P. 172, Jean Domarchi.
Author of a study on George Cukor in the Editions Seghers series, and a contributor to *Cahiers du Cinéma.*

P. 173, Palais Royal.
A Parisian theater with a long and varied history from 1783 to the present. Since 1830 it has been the home of vaudeville.

THE DESTINY OF JEAN GABIN
From *Radio-Cinéma-Télévision,* October 1, 1950

P. 177, Tino Rossi.

Born Corsica, 1907. Popular operetta star and film actor. Created a new style of singing popular songs in contrast to the intellectual style of most French *chansonniers*. He was immensely popular and had fan clubs all over France. Luis Mariani was an imitator of Rossi in material and style.

RELATED READINGS

Aristarco, G. *Storia delle teoriche del film.* Einaudi, Torino, 1960.

Ayfre, A. *Conversion aux images?* Editions du Cerf, Paris, 1964.

Bandelier, A., and Giros, P. *Amédee Ayfre.* Editions Fleures, Paris, 1968.

Chiarini, L. *Il film nella battaglia delle idee.* Fratelli Bocca Editore, Milano, 1954.

Farber, M., ed. *Philosophic Thought in France and the United States.* S.U.N.Y. Press, Albany, 1968 (2d ed.).

Heiney, D. *America in Modern Italian Literature.* Rutgers, New Brunswick, N. J., 1964.

Maritain, J. *Structure of Poetry* [*Art et scolastique*]. Philosophical Library, New York, 1953.

Mitry, J. *Esthéthique et psychologie du cinéma* (2 vols). Editions Universitares, Paris, 1963–1965.

Moix, C. *La Pensée d'Emmanuel Mounier.* Editions du Seuil, Paris, 1960.

Mounier, E. *Oeuvres,* Vols. I-IV. Editions du Seuil, Paris, 1961–1962.

Cahiers du Cinéma, 1951–1959.

Cinéthique, January–February 1970.

Esprit, January 1949–1957; May 1959.

Revista del cinema italiano, No. 3, March 1954.

Temps Modernes, Les, December 1946-December 1952; October 1970.

INDEX

INDEX

Index

Index

Index